The Private Life
of the Minister's Wife

The Private Life of the Minister's Wife

Betty J. Coble

Broadman Press
Nashville, Tennessee

4269-35
ISBN: 0-8054-6935-4

Dewey Decimal Classification: 253.2

Subject heading: MINISTERS' WIVES

Library of Congress Catalog Card Number: 81-65385

Printed in the United States of America

This book is dedicated
to the memory of my husband who for
thirty-two years gave me the privilege of
being the wife of a minister.

Preface

Mirror, mirror, in the hall—as I reflect on myself, I really like what I see—sometimes. At other times, I wish she were someone else.

I have only a vague idea of what is expected of me. For me, this role confusion creates a blurry image. The shape of my role comes from all sources—the church, family, and friends. Even strangers outside the church have their ideas of who this special woman is.

The images of a minister's wife are as varied as the individuals who form them. To one I must be outgoing, enthusiastic, well groomed, intelligent, tireless, unruffled, a teacher, musician, hostess, friend, counselor, nurse, and athlete. To another I must be quiet, always in the background, and neat but demure. I should never offer an opinion or be in the forefront and should always be guided by what others need. I should look the part (whatever that means). And on and on the description goes.

There are those who feel that a minister's wife is a "super" individual who never has to prepare for anything she does. To them I have answers without study. Their rationale is that living with a "man of God" makes everything easier for me, and my life runs smoothly all of the time. How do I tell them who I really am?

Opinions of what the wife of a minister should be haunt women who are ministers' wives; these opinions even frighten those who are asked to consider the position. For over thirty years I have been a wife to a husband who served the Lord in a local church as pastor and in the Air Force as a chaplain. Many times I have reevaluated my commitment first made as a young woman in love who said, "I want to be *your* wife." While I have found that being a wife in full view of a congregation gives many extra opportunities for service, it is hazardous at times. Let me share some practical ideas that have helped me to be a *person*, not only a bearer of several labels.

Many people have encouraged me to be myself. Some of my best friends who are ministers' wives have helped me to work through difficult situations in my life, giving me courage to be an individual. I have taken advantage of every group meeting of ministers' wives from a local level to a national level. My church has allowed me the privilege of service where I have chosen. By this, I do not mean everyone has liked me or thought I was where I belonged. My husband helped me learn to keep my priorities in order, but I did not appreciate his information every time.

In struggling to find my own identity I have found a very fulfilling life as a minister's wife. Through the meetings I have attended, the surveys I have studied, the close friends who have shared with me, and my own struggles, I see a minister's wife's needs as very basic.

There are resources available to meet her needs. There are answers to the questions that confront her. There are a number of new books available that will help her to see how common her problems are. Each book helps with new insights.

My purpose in this book is to be of help by discussing some areas of resource, opportunity, and need in the life of a woman married to a man who ministers in a religious vocation—whether the man be pastor, minister of education, music, youth, senior adults, chaplain, or any other leader in ministry.

When I began this manuscript I was happily teaching, writing, and speaking as a minister's wife. As I conclude my last draft I no longer bear the label minister's wife, but widow. As one of the congregation, now I have an even greater appreciation and admiration for you. I also see in sharper focus the problems, challenges, and joys I had experienced throughout the years.

Contents

1
Labeled: Minister's Wife

Are you a minister's wife or the wife of a minister? Many ministers' wives have had someone say to them, "You don't look like a minister's wife." Recently, while leading a seminar of young ministers' wives, I asked if that statement made them feel complimented or guilty. Overwhelmingly they responded, "Complimented."

They felt complimented because they did not fit into the drab stereotype role that many accept as how a minister's wife is to look and act.

There were a few persons in the seminar who felt guilty because they were not measuring up to the standard that others were holding up before them. Others evidenced guilt because they failed to conform to a self-imposed image.

Not every minister's wife has difficulty wearing that label. Women who are comfortable with this label have found their own identity, taken charge of their own lives, and found their place of service. Most of these fortunate women have had someone to help them form a positive point of view. For each one who has found her way, however, there is one who is groping and in need of encouragement.

For those who find the label "minister's wife" difficult to wear most or some of the time, we will examine *why* it becomes stressful from time to time.

I have often heard this said to young women who are dedicated to the Lord and serving faithfully: "You would make a good minister's wife." Many single young women dream of such a place of honor and position. They see the minister's wife as one who has life all put together with no problems *(has a perfect husband),* a position next to her husband *(a co-worker or a team member),* with the love of all the congregation directed toward her *(never lonely),* and having every opportunity to serve the Lord *(in any category she wishes).*

Other young women I have talked with say, "No way. Not me." They see the minister's wife as a person without a husband *(always serving somewhere else)*, pushed aside *(rarely recognized as an individual)*, with everyone's problems stacked on top of her *(with very little time of her own)*, and being responsible for every job that someone else doesn't want to do *(just not that talented)*.

Despite all the emphasis today on being your own person, there is still an outdated mold of a minister's wife in the minds of most people. Those preconceived ideas are passed on subtly and subconsciously from generation to generation. When asked directly, most people are somewhat ashamed that they try to mold the minister's wife's role; they confess it really is not right. Yet they still feel she is different. Others are very adamant about *how* she should be different.

Although we know how impossible it is to live up to unrealistic expectations, we are at least obligated to seek some answers regarding the minister's wife's role. How others see us should not be our primary concern. How we see ourselves is our priority here. This eliminates the unnatural behavior of trying to fit into a stereotype. There are degrees of conformity that we all submit to, but we must give ourselves permission to be the person God wants us to be.

There is a difference between idealism and reality for all of us. For instance, many persons are shocked by the difference in how they thought marriage would be and how it really is. In addition to the normal adjustments in a marriage, it should not be surprising to realize the overwhelming adjustments involved in being a minister's wife.

Every person wears several labels during a lifetime—person, female, daughter, sister, friend, student, Christian, church member, wife, mother, daughter-in-law, grandmother, widow, and on and on we could go. A label is a convenient generalized classification. All of these labels have a general definition that is accepted by everyone. The popular label of a grandmother illustrates this point. She has an image of being a person who is always ready to show you the latest pictures of her grandchildren. She is eager to tell you all of the clever things they have done or said. But popular image will not suffice as a foundation for lasting relationships. Interpersonal experiences are necessary for one to have positive associations with the labels. When a person has a loving grandmother, he associates the word *grand-mother* with warmth and love and a mental image of his grand-mother's face.

One of the ways to find happiness and fulfillment in being the wife of a minister is to take the labels you have chosen and define them for yourself. To take the previously defined label of "minister's wife" and to try to squeeze yourself into it or reshape yourself to fit into it is to contradict God's word. God designed individuals to be distinctively original, having the freedom to direct their own lives. To accept someone else's worn-out definition of "minister's wife" is to forfeit privilege and choice.

Some wives reject the label. They set out to prove their indepen-dence and to rebel just to be different. The wife can experience a lot of misery by not defining the label. By resisting other people's defini-tion, these wives are refusing to make a commitment to the direction in which they plan to go.

There are so many fields of ministry. There are ministries on a full-time commitment basis, but not a part-time schedule. There is no way that one book can speak to each individual need. There are also contrasting geographical locations that call for different appli-cations of ministering. There are the varying sizes of congregations. Even age is a factor. The fact still remains that in each particular life situation, only the woman involved can define the label "minister's wife."

There are times when a minister's wife feels that her predicament is the result of circumstances or someone else's decision. A closer look backward will probably reveal that it was possible to have gone an-other way. Choices were made. She chose to be a wife, but perhaps not to be the wife of a minister. In many cases husbands enter the ministry after marriage. Many wives feel like outsiders because they did not sense a call into the ministry along with their husband's call-ing. Other wives feel a call and find a bit of resentment at being classified in a secondary position. This is a hurting area in particular for the wife who sees "minister's wife" as a position of service for which she has educated herself academically. She sees her position as equally important to the advancement of the kingdom, only without the recognition. I have spoken to a number of foreign missionary wives who have been frustrated because they had not defined their own label as a wife serving on a foreign field with her husband.

The labels worn are to be defined in relationship to the persons who make them possible. When the label minister's wife is defined, keep in mind that you are the wife of a person whose profession is ministering. So the real challenge is to define "wife" in relationship to the uniqueness of your husband.

In composing a definition to a label, you need to keep four things in mind. First, *take an in-depth look at who you are and what you want out of your life.* Sometimes when you are asked to state who you are, you tend to look at who you are not or to focus on only one area of your life. Every wife would profit by writing down all the labels she wears. Labels have different values to each of us. Since some things are more important to us than to others, a total picture can more readily be seen by listing your labels in the order of importance to you. There are times when a label is difficult to wear and times when it is a joy to wear.

Where are *you* going in life? Sometimes this is answered, "Wherever my husband goes." This question is not marriage or family based. Each of you needs to determine where you are going in your present circumstances. This gives you direction. It also helps you to become responsible *for* yourself. How will you know when you have arrived if you do not know where you are going?

A second thing to keep in mind in defining labels is that *there are choices to be made every day of your life.* When we continue to live our lives looking back to what might have been or dreaming about what could be, we miss the opportunity of living today. As we seek to live in the present, we need to personalize God's Word. He is not writing to groups or individuals who must function perfectly before his promises are valid. In fact, the majority of the Bible is addressed to us for personal application. Many of the miracles Christ performed were on a one-to-one basis. We readily accept the fact that we can only become children of God on an individual basis, but God's concern for us as individuals is often overlooked. God is concerned that we be the recipients of the abundant life that he came to give all of us. He wants us to experience happiness, joy, and fulfillment. Choices must be made from what is available to you. I believe there is room for abundant living where each child of God is stationed.

A third consideration in defining labels is to *discover the main source of discontent* if there is discontent. When we are unhappy, it is easy to say that it does not matter or that everyone is unhappy. We tend to ignore our unhappiness instead of honestly evaluating it to correct it. Much unhappiness comes when we depend on others to make us happy. Happiness comes from within. As we find those things that bring fulfillment to us and accomplish them, we gain purpose. Purpose satisfies, and happiness becomes the by-product.

Added pressures are experienced when we fear that we are not living up to the expectations of others. Fear often causes unhappiness in an otherwise happy situation. Hebrews 13:5b-6 says, " 'I will never desert you, nor will I ever forsake you,' so that we confidently say, 'The Lord is my helper, I will not be afraid. What shall man do to me?' " (NASB). Fear robs a person's identity and energy. It causes comparison of ourselves with others, which often leads to trying to be like them or having them be like us. Fear is a form of giving the control of your life to someone else. The other person's idea of what your life is supposed to be is being imposed upon you.

Resentment is often a source of discontent, and we usually don't recognize it. We often fail to heed the teachings of Ephesians 4:26-32 with regard to anger. "Be angry, and yet do not sin; do not let the sun go down on your anger, and do not give the devil an opportunity" (vv. 26-27, NASB). We have misunderstood the term *controlled anger* to mean that we are not to be angry or that we are just to forget about it. The Scriptures say that we are to resolve our anger in a constructive way. If we do not deal with today's anger today, then tomorrow it will become resentment and eventually develop into bitterness. Ephesians 4:31 teaches us that bitterness, wrath, anger, clamor, slander, and malice are the result of not taking care of anger daily. This is accomplished by loving, caring, and forgiving just like Christ is doing for us (v. 32).

There are many other sources of discontent that could be listed.

The point is that you must decide what yours is in order to better define your labels. A better label definition could alleviate much discontent.

How you view the label is the fourth consideration. A negative attitude toward the label to be defined will cause you difficulty. Many times when we are happy we feel there is no need to define a label. This is not true. An undefined label leads to a certain amount of confusion in life. It also leaves little room for success.

A few months following my husband's death I was asked to consider a church staff position. In my grief and confusion of my new label of a businesswoman—now totally responsible for myself—I found I could not give intelligent consideration to a job by only looking at the disadvantages. Days before the interview I became more and more perplexed as I looked at all of the reasons I could not possibly take the position. I decided to spend the last few days listing all of the advantages I could think of. Of course, during the interview the pastor listed all of the advantages of the position. It took only a short time to decide that the job was not for me. Despite all of the pluses, there was not enough for me to work with.

A minister's wife must view her label from the advantages of her position instead of the disadvantages in order to have materials with which to work. To try to build anything with materials you do not have causes failure. It would be beneficial to list all of the advantages of being the wife of your husband. Defining a label says you have decided who you are and what you are willing to give in building a relationship.

As you think through what you are willing to give, you have something definite to offer. Titus 2:3-5 states that older women are responsible for teaching younger women. We need to look to the Scripture and find all that we can in order to define our labels by God's Word. God states many things for us to do as his children. The doers are the builders.

There is a difference of opinion about whether a divine call to be a minister's wife is necessary. Many times in both large and small groups I have heard this matter discussed. Pros and cons are about equally divided. The issue does raise some probing questions. Are there any instructions from the Lord on this? Is the call of the minister's wife to *any* man who might be a minister or to a *specific* man? Is the call to a way of life or to follow the Lord? Can God's leadership divide a husband and wife and send them in separate directions? Is the priority of emphasis of service to God of top priority in the church or in the marriage?

The confusion regarding God's direction includes both choices for ministry and changes in the ministerial role. Women whose husbands have changed their area of ministering sometimes become very dissatisfied because they are not being allowed to carry out their calling. Is God's leadership causing a separation? How much say does the wife have in deciding where the area of service is to be? Are we confusing the word *called* with *commitment* to God's way for our life? Are we committed to a position or to Christ and his daily direction?

"I am not happy with where I am. I can no longer fill my calling as a pastor's wife since my husband is in his new ministering position. I really feel we are out of the Lord's will." These statements were shared with me by a distraught minister's wife. I asked her to take time to examine her calling, then to share it with me. Her narrative began with a pastor's wife who had strongly influenced her in her formative years. She had admired the pastor's wife and decided she wanted to be that dedicated in helping others.

When she fell in love with Gary, she decided she could carry out her commitment to Christ as his wife because he was a ministerial student at the time. In her search for a definition of her call to be a pastor's wife, she realized that her call was a commitment to Christ. She said to me, "I have a burden lifted from me. I am free to serve and carry out that commitment where I am." It's good to take inventory of yourself and see if you are committed to a position or to Christ. Our call is to service.

A role is usually stereotyped and may be impersonal. God has not designed a set path that is inflexible. He has given us the privilege of choosing a mate and a pattern by which that relationship is to be built. When we choose relationship over role we are recognizing the person as more valuable than the position. This emphasizes the importance of our mate. When we gather vital current information on where we are today as persons, we become more aware of what we have to contribute to a relationship.

Is survival enough, or is there more to life? As a young wife I could look around and see that almost everyone was surviving, but many looked as if they wished they were not. Today there is more emphasis on fullness of life. Hence, more and more ministers' wives are saying, "I cannot handle this position any longer." There is little criticism, if any, when a woman decides to change jobs because she is not satisfied where she is employed. There is too little consideration for the person when a minister's wife resigns her *position as wife of the church* to become the *wife of her husband.*

A friend shared her doubts with me about being able to meet the expectations of a minister's wife. The wise words of her mother put the situation in perspective: "It is not easy to be anybody's wife." This turned my friend's concern from the role to the relationship, and she married the young man. They recently celebrated their thirtieth wedding anniversary and are enjoying a happy marriage.

Each of the following chapters discusses a label that influences the role of a "minister's wife." Each chapter opens up a new facet of her total person. In defining these labels she is enabled to be more in charge of her own life. This results in a more comfortable relationship with others. She also has a definite mission and feels confident that God's will is unfolding in her life.

2
The Person I Am Is Me

To define "minister's wife" for yourself, it is necessary to begin with the person you are. As you reflect, the image you see is who you *are*—not who you should be or who you hope to become.

The joy of discovering who you are as a person is scheduled by God to continue for a lifetime and perhaps throughout eternity. Who you *are* today, where you are, the way you are is your building material to become what you want to be.

What is meant by being *you?* Some things that are being said by the media and feminist leaders about assertion and aggression can be damaging if they disregard others. To be assertive is to be positive and confident in a persistent way. In order to be assertive, you must like the person you are. An aggressive person, sometimes thought of in a negative way, is ready and willing to take issue easily.

God did not give us the *right* to crush other people in pursuit of *ourselves.* If we pressure others to gain control of our lives or of their lives, we are manipulative. We are not to live as if we are the only people who count. Assertion and aggression, wrongly used, can eventually mean isolation and loneliness. The wife who says, "I don't care how you feel or what you think; I am going to do what I want to do" is forgetting all former commitments. Her main goal is self-gratification. People refuse to share with a person who is seeking control. They pull away to protect themselves from being run over, maimed, or emotionally killed.

How special is each minister's wife according to God? Each one's life was created by God; she was born to parents who were given the responsibility of training and loving; she was sought out with God's love to be one of his children.

One of God's designs for you is to be female. In some circles today, you may feel that you need to apologize for the fact that God chose to make you a female person. In other groups you hear that women are being given advantages because they are female. There are hours of dialogue on equal rights. Many times in such discussions the issues are confused because the discussion becomes a battle of which sex is superior.

The Bible teaches us that God does not value one person over another. He does say if we are going to change the quality of our existence to have "abundant life," we need to understand what we have to work *with* and what relationships we are going to work *on.* For each relationship, there are basic principles that must be understood.

A good place to begin sorting through who you are is to accept the female person that God has made you without regret or arrogant pride. *Feminine* according to the dictionary means "a female, a woman, the female sex." Yet there is a real effort by some to make feminine be determined by what you wear, the way you talk, how dependent you are, or how domestic you act. This concept of femininity is programmed into us by descriptions of the pretty, petite (5'2"), neatly dressed, soft-spoken young woman. Anything less is unfeminine. Female person is the beginning of your identity. At birth the infant is identified as female and given a name that helps to further identify her.

In the Scriptures there is the closest possible relationship between a person and his or her name. God gave Israel her name and called her his people. There is significance attached to a name in a family and to the person who bears it. The greatest kind of care is given to the selecting of a child's name. The continuing of a family name, or the fondness for a name because of the association with a person, helps to determine the name to be given to a new baby.

I enjoyed the new experience of helping select names for our family's first three grandchildren. We brainstormed each time we were together, since all three families were searching for names at the same time. Names were acceptable because of sound, meaning, or association. I was asked by an acquaintance what my first grandson's name was to be; and I gladly responded, "At this time, his name is to be Ian Thomas." The response was, "I don't like that name. Please try to talk Tom and Linda out of that name." My reply was, "It is their child, and it is their privilege to name him."

Each person begins very early to identify with his name. Loneliness and questions of one's worth come when there is a lack of usage of one's name. Recently, as I was introduced to a woman, I remarked, "You do not look like a Jane." She was rather startled as she said, "Jane is not my real name, but it is what my family has chosen to call me. All of my life I have felt strange being called by a name that was not mine. It has always made me feel there was something wrong with me." Our names are important to us. Nicknames or pet names are used in families as endearments. "This is my poopsie, dollie, or babee." Such names can even become a source of embarrassment when used outside the family circle or used into adulthood.

When a person is identified by a title instead of her name, there is a recognition of her position but none of personal relationship. Many ministers' wives are introduced with: "This is our minister's wife" (no use of her name). This practice is not only poor etiquette, but it proves that there is a lack of identity on the part of the woman except by her role. This impersonal treatment by the congregation contributes to the isolation and loneliness of many ministers' wives.

To hear one's name spoken provokes warmth, friendship, and interest in her as an individual. If you are not presently called by a name of your choosing, decide what name you wish to be called. With some people in the congregation Mrs. Blank will be most appropriate, but with others there is a real need to be on a first-name basis. Put people at ease. Tell them what you prefer to be called. This can be done on a one-to-one basis, or your selected name can be given when requested in a group.

Some ministers' wives establish a Mrs. Preacher or a Mrs. Educational Director to keep people at a safe distance. If you are more comfortable with that sort of name it is yours to decide, but I would ask that you examine the limited involvement you are indicating by allowing a role to be substituted for your name. Friendships are not established between positions, but between people.

How do you see yourself? Are you a valuable, talented female who is content with her status in life?

Loving others is very closely tied to the value an individual places on herself. I have spent a number of years working with youth. Many of them had problems in relating to others resulting from a very poor self-esteem. When I was able to help a person like herself, the problem with peers disappeared. I have also found this true with adults.

Most people related to Christian service are striving to love and care for those with whom they are involved. A minister's wife is quite familiar with many Scriptures; at least she has heard them repeated enough that she has a general guide in her life for loving others. Jesus gave us a precedent for loving: " 'Which is the great commandment in the Law?' And he said to him, 'You shall love the Lord your God with all your heart, and with all your soul, and with all your mind. This is the great and foremost commandment. And the second is like it, You shall love your neighbor as yourself. On these two commandments depend the whole Law and the Prophets' " (Matt. 22:36-40, NASB). The command is to love God with total self. That is possible because "We love, because He first loved us" (1 John 4:19, NASB). The acceptance of his love for you is necessary in order to have it to give to another. If love were a liquid, most of us would not have a container to carry it in if it meant we must take it to ourselves first.

James called the royal law "You shall love your neighbor as yourself" (Jas. 2:8, NASB).

After I spoke to a group of senior citizens on "Liking You" one evening, a man came by to tell me, "I have seen something this evening that has always bothered me. I could never figure out why I have always had a criticism to offer about everyone. Now I realize I have never been pleased with myself. I could not tell you one thing I like about me." What a pity when a person spends a lifetime criticizing what God has given him to work with.

Paul admonished the Romans to keep God's commandments: "You shall love your neighbor as yourself" (Rom. 13:9, NASB). In another letter, this time to the Galatians, he said, "For the whole Law is fulfilled in one word, in the statement, 'You shall love your neighbor as yourself' " (Gal. 5:14, NASB). Are we afraid to let God love us? God is the source of our love; we draw from him to give to others. The minister's wife who tries to be patient with everyone yet scolds herself anytime she has a contrary thought is not letting God love her. Therefore, she does not have much love to give to others.

This command has been in effect since God spoke to Moses: "But you shall love your neighbor as yourself" (Lev. 19:18, NASB). The woman who is very helpful to the sick but drags herself to a meeting when her head aches until she can hardly see is not loving herself. She is using service as a substitute for love. Resentment is her reward.

There is a right and wrong kind of love for oneself. The right kind is kept in the order that Jesus places it: first, to love God with your total being; and second, to accept the fact that God created you, endowed you, values you, loves you, and gives you the opportunity to accept or reject that love. These are two of the most valuable foundations of self-esteem. If his love is rejected, then we might as well forget trying to love others. Without Christ we cannot manufacture enough love to last through our lifetime of relationships.

God pleads with believers through his Word and through his Holy Spirit to accept his love. It is provided by him, but it must be used on ourselves first. We do not appreciate something given to us that is not valued by the giver. The greatest hindrance to the Christian testimony today is not taking seriously God's love for us as individuals. He loves you. Being kind to the members of the congregation yet not taking a day off for yourself makes for attitudes such as, "Why do others expect me to serve in places they are not willing to serve?"

One of our greatest fears as believers is that we will think too highly of ourselves. This subject is addressed by the apostle Paul.

The "lovers of self" spoken of in 2 Timothy 3:2 are persons who are interested in their own way without regard for Christ. This is a wrong kind of self-love. A word study of the wrong kind of self-love is examined in the book *Man: Responsible and Caring* by Harold H. Coble (my late husband). He states:

> The Bible does speak of a wrong kind of self-love (2 Tim. 3:1-5). Paul's use of "philautoi"—lovers of self—in this passage is the only New Testament use of this word. (Nor is it used in the Septuagint.) Obviously from the statements following in verses 2-5, the apostle is using lovers of self in a bad sense. This sense is further indicated in verse 3 where Paul speaks of the *philautoi* as being "without natural affection." Paul indicates elsewhere (Eph. 5:28) it is right and natural for a man to love himself. Of course, this doesn't mean self-centeredness, rather the opposite is true in the right kind of self-love (p. 48).

Love "does not seek its own" (1 Cor. 13:5b, NASB). There are many places in Scripture where we are told to love ourselves. We have a Bible full of examples of God's love for us. A minister's wife accepting God's love for herself removes the need for manipulating others. Constant approval from others is not necessary. She knows God loves her.

A wrong kind of self-love would be selfishness, too much concern with one's own welfare or interests and having little or no concern for others. Liking oneself is not narcissistic — an exaggerated sense of self-importance with a lack of sustained positive regard for others. Dr. Otto Kernberg, medical director of Cornell Medical Center, New Yor`., said in *Psychology Today,* "A narcissist does not really love herself at all; she actually holds herself in low-esteem." The attitude of having to stoop down to care for another person makes the wrong person seem unworthy. The arrogant one has the real need. She is trying to give out of her emptiness.

In an effort to compensate for the one who is looking down on others, some seek to delete self from all involvement or credit. The attempt is made by removing the "I" from sin and saying we have no sin or removing the "I" from pride and saying we have no pride. If this theory would work we must remember that by removing the "I" out of life, service, commitment, marriage, and Christianity, we would have no one to work with. The "I" is God's creation. We are endowed by him, instructed by him, loved by him, sought by him, saved by him, and empowered by him.

Healthy love of self comes as a result of loving God and accepting God's love for us on a personal basis. A good barometer for self-esteem is the way you accept a compliment. When others see value in you, your gracious acknowledgment says you know you are one of God's unique children. There is no comparison being made. Being uncomfortable with compliments is being critical of yourself and rejecting the other person's feelings.

Accepting yourself as you are and liking what God has given you to work with gives you a very necessary tool for building a better relationship with God and with others.

How do you see yourself most of the time? Shy or aggressive, talented or with no talent, positive or negative, happy or unhappy, pretty or ugly, slim or fat, organized or confused, strong or weak, graceful or clumsy, charming or a bore, attractive or drab, active or inactive, educated or dumb, wise or stupid, truthful or dishonest, polite or rude, cheerful or moody, tactful or brash, cordial or unfriendly, loving or cold?

The way you see yourself has much to do with your happiness and your fulfillment. All of us have blue Mondays from time to time but depressions of greater depths are also a common experience. In a recent article for Christian counselors I found a simple analysis on what causes depression. The writer, Maurice E. Wagner, basically said that *depression begins with criticism of oneself.* The second step is *to blame others or your circumstances* for the way you feel. The final step is to feel as if there is *no hope.* As I have looked at myself and as I have observed other women, I find these three steps very valid. *The first step down is self-criticism.*

One Sunday morning as we backed out of our driveway on our way to church, I casually remarked to my husband, "We are really not very good neighbors." After about a minute of thought, my husband replied, "You can place that guilt on yourself if you want to, but I refuse to accept it for myself. I feel that I give all of the time to our neighbors that I have to give." As I thought about it, I was placing an unrealistic standard on myself for what a good neighbor should be. My ideal for the moment was the TV coffee lady who drops in and shares and solves all your hostess problems. I took inventory of my relationship with the people who lived around me and found that I did give them a fair amount of time. I soon realized that I was putting myself down. This harsh self-criticism is where most discouragement begins.

Criticism is not a motivator; it places guilt on us. This is how we move so easily into the second step of depression, which many times comes by the comparison of ourselves with, "I do as well as so-and-so and better than most." Or we can come to the place of blaming our circumstances. "If I had more time or if others did not require so much of my time, I could be a better neighbor."

Criticism is destructive. We are looking at what we *do not have* and not *what we have* to work with. There is no way we can tear down and build up at the same time. Criticism can come in a very subtle form. It may be no more than doing a task for another person when he has not asked for your assistance.

Because of an experience I had in my teens, I spent many years feeling reticent about giving my Christian testimony. I had tried to share with Joyce, a school friend of mine. She was from a large family who had no interest in Christianity. Through our friendship and her aunt's encouragement, she began attending Sunday School and church. After a special service one night I was talking with her about accepting Jesus; an older woman came up and pushed me aside with, "Let me tell her. You don't know how." Joyce was polite and listened but did not choose to become a Christian. I lost contact with her after her aunt's death, but at that time she was still not a believer.

I already had doubts about my ability to tell her what she needed to know. Basically, I agreed with the criticism of the older woman. For many years I did not dare share my own testimony because I felt I did not know how. I did not attempt to convince others to become Christians until I realized that my testimony was just that—my testimony. It is valid because it is mine.

The person who is always missing the mark in her own eyes finds it easy to agree with others who criticize her. John 8:17 and Deuteronomy 19:15b emphasize that it takes two or three witnesses to establish a truth. Does this not also happen if the words are negative? A woman who is critical of the way she looks is devastated by a derogatory comment from another person. She agrees with the other person about the negative statement about herself.

If her opinion of herself is not based on perfection, the negative comment can be accepted as the other person's opinion. If a friend says she does not like you in green, does that indicate to you that you should never wear green? No, she is only telling you what she likes. Evaluate all comments by seeing yourself as a valuable person, not a perfect person, who must try to please everyone.

Do you have a standard for yourself that says you should have succeeded already in accomplishments, knowledge, and growth? You must remember that you are only on your way in the Christian walk and must give yourself room for growth.

As you are living out your life, plan to develop those areas where you have opportunities. If you want to try teaching—substitute for an age group you have interest in. If teaching does not interest you, choose something that is important to you. See everything you do as a means to experience some growing. Sometimes what you discover is that that particular service is not for you. We all have abilities to see areas of need that others are not aware of.

Since Christ gives us time to mature and become like him, why do we look around to start comparing ourselves with others to see how we are doing? Comparison of yourself with another is like saying an orange and an apple should look and taste alike because they are both fruit. What we should look to others for is encouragement, not comparison. One minister's wife looks at the other minister's wife and it seems that she has so much talent or education; everything is so easy in her life. We say, "If I just had everything that she has, I would have it all together, with ease." What we need to realize is that the only way we can really know what is going on in her life is to be living her life. She has needs too. Learn from her. Do not compare yourself with her.

Many times the comparison is not being done by the minister's wife herself, but by those around her. Probably no situation puts her more on guard than the statement "Our former minister's wife always . . . " The ghosts of the past are frightening until we find that they are not real. You are their minister's wife. Learn to compliment the former minister's wife along with them, and do not try to compare yourself with her. She is gone. You are there. Be yourself. That is really what church members need. It is all you can be anyway. You cannot look in a mirror and see someone else. Trying to be another person sets you up for failure and cheats the congregation out of knowing another one of God's special people.

The ability to love, share, and continue to care is based on how valuable one feels she is to God. A person thinking of herself as having little value is criticizing the abilities God has given her to work with. This attitude about herself will automatically become the standard she places on others. The apostle Paul, in writing to the Philippians, said, "For I am confident of this very thing, that He who began a good work in you will perfect it until the day of Christ Jesus" (Phil. 1:6, NASB). Christ sets the value and gives a lifetime to complete the project given. There is struggle involved in being confident in God's value of personhood when you are talking about you.

God is giving you an opportunity to win people to Christ by your life-style and by your boldness. It takes courage to like oneself. Being yourself, as a believer, makes Christ believable. Being yourself makes you comfortable so that you see the needs of others and have the energy to reach out to them. I listened in on a conversation next to me recently and heard a woman say, "You may not see our minister's wife in the choir; but if you ever have a personal grief, she is there to comfort you. I can't tell you how many times I have arrived at a home and she has already been there. She is one of a kind." These women were appreciating the uniqueness of their minister's wife.

The apostle Paul said in Philippians 2:1-7 that a good attitude is required for effective service. What this is saying to me is that since Christ is real, let us encourage one another. To consider others better than yourself and be unselfish can only be done honestly if you rightly value yourself before God.

Jesus, knowing who he was and where he was going, was able to do a task as menial as washing the disciples' feet (John 13:3-5). The illustration given us is that we should be gauging ourselves by Christ's example. Christ knew who he was—he disciplined himself even to go to his death for us to pay for our sins (Phil. 2:5-9, NASB). Therefore, verse 12, "Work out your salvation" (schedules of priorities by your value system) in relation to what God commands in his Word—not what others say it should be for you.

It is easy for others to try to schedule your time by their needs because they could not accomplish all they intended. Humility calls for knowing who you are in relationship to God. Appreciating what God has given you is accepting his love. Now you are equipped to value others. Esteeming others better than yourself does not mean you are worthless. It means being able to compliment without comparison. We only see the value and worthwhileness of others through clear eyes unmarred by self-criticism.

Thank God for who you are. Be specific. Tell him how you appreciate what he has given you to work with. This necessitates being able to name some of the materials we have to work with: for example, your enthusiasm, quietness, kindness, hospitality, friendliness, attractiveness, or other attributes.

Let's stand together and see the good in each believer. So a fellow Christian doesn't like your new outfit because she thinks the skirt is too long. She doesn't have to wear it. That is fine. You like it. You wear it and enjoy yourself by giving her the same freedom you want — to be herself and have her own taste — as ridiculous as her taste may seem to you.

How you see God is determined largely by the relationship you had with your parents as a child. Most of our parents emphasized the merit system. Our value was determined by how well we performed as compared with others. We have been taught not to be competitive. In school, a child who does not measure up to the norm is many times labeled an underachiever. These early experiences leave little room for the individual. *God's Word majors on the individual.*

In a seminar on parenting I attended at Rosemead Graduate School of Psychology, Dr. Clyde Narramore said that in his years of counseling he had discovered two things that give a child a negative view of God and of self. One is parents who try to motivate their child to perform better by criticism. The other is parents who love their child on a performance basis.

I have observed that a person with a negative view of God will major on the punishment of God instead of the love of God.

The discipline of God is very evident in the Scripture, and it proves his love. Discipline is a training that develops self-control, character, orderliness, and efficiency in the believer's life. Punishment, however, means to cause to undergo pain, loss, or suffering for a wrongdoing. Punishment is reserved for those who reject God, for unbelievers.

God's requirements are that we believe in him by accepting his provision for our sins in the person of Christ and that we find abundant life by following his commandments, which constitute his will for us. The main commandment to all persons is to love God, love self, and love others. The individual is free to select the place and way of carrying out God's commands. Love is received from God when we value ourselves as he values us. It is received from others when we accept their love as they choose to give it to us. When we are willing to give love to others without requirements, we are loving God.

God is for us. Everyone else can be against us, but he continues to be for us. Nothing can separate us from his love for us. His love is the strongest motivating force there is. We need to relax and enjoy it more often so that we will have some to give away.

If you doubt the value of each person, I would challenge you to begin to search the Scripture in your study time and to see the wonder with which we were created, the planning that was put into our salvation. God has stated just what we need to know to build a close relationship to him, husband, children, and other Christians. He has demonstrated how we are to reach out to those that do not know him. He has commanded us to love. He gave us a detailed description of love in 1 Corinthians 13. He has also demonstrated love. He has loved us with the kind of love he asks us to give to others.

God is in the salvage business. He does not junk his wrecks but helps them to take what they have and adds his dimension of forgiveness and restoration.

From the beginning of the human race, God has dealt with us as individuals. In the Garden of Eden, God required Eve to be answerable to him for herself. He made Adam responsible for himself. The serpent was also accountable for himself.

God has had plenty of reasons to deal with us as a group and destroy us all. Because of his unconditional love, he gives us the chance to restore our relationship with him and move on from there. Some seem to look at this restoration as a change to all they are going to become, instead of treating it as a new beginning from where they are. A young minister's wife who is overly concerned with where she should be is usually wasting her time where she is.

Read 1 Corinthians 13:4-7 to see how God looks at you. He loves from a positive viewpoint, looking at you as one who is forgiven in Christ Jesus. He is not critical of you. God's love is an unconditional commitment to an undeserving person. (It is not won by our performance.) It is not how nice you are or how many good deeds you perform that determines God's love.

We need to understand what true humility is. It is freedom from a pride that makes comparisons. A humble person has a right opinion of herself in relationship to God; is not arrogant but teachable; is not a braggart (a bragger is a comparer); is not pushy (is pleased to help others, not to receive their approval). All of these qualifications indicate that a person respects herself as an individual and sees value in herself in relationship to God rather than in comparison to others.

Humility is a quality that is sought after in a wrong direction many times. A woman classified as a humble person is often described as a person who does not recognize good qualities in herself and who is always putting down anything that she might do. This is humiliation, not humility. I have a minister-friend who is always joking about the book he is going to write about how he achieved humility.

When God spoke to Mary, saying that she had been chosen to be the mother of Jesus, she showed her confidence in God and her self-esteem as she expressed her joy of being used of God. There would have been no room for her utterance of praise if she had been questioning her worth. God said she was highly favored. She accepted God's evaluation of her (see Luke 1:46-55). A minister's wife hinders what God could do through her when she spends time judging how much better others could serve than she would be able to serve.

There is much use of Matthew 16:24 to justify the demeaning of the individual. The phrase "let him deny himself" means to disregard one's interest that is in conflict with Christ and to follow him. This has nothing to do with the worth of the individual. We are being told who is to be the leader. If we follow Christ, then he is to lead. We are not given the option to go in our own direction and still say we are following. The way to follow Christ is to love those who are unlovely. An example of a denying of self in this situation would be to be kind to those who mistreat you.

In order to know what qualities you have for use in ministering to others, it is necessary for you to be acquainted with yourself and your worth before God. Preparation of a dinner for a group of people calls for inventory of what is on hand and a trip to buy what is needed. Even a skilled cook cannot serve dinner if there is nothing to prepare. Trying to serve others from a *nothing* opinion of oneself is just as futile.

Part of the frustration of identity is the fallacy of waiting for others to tell us who we are. A minister's wife has an abundance of this kind of information. Some see her as OK with lots of abilities, while others would like to completely remodel her. God places each person in charge of her (one and only) life. As director of my life, I must make the plans for where I want to go, schedule the events, make changes when necessary, and be responsible for my choices.

Some people feel that to be director of their own lives they must get off in a secluded place to be alone so they are not influenced by others. Others feel they must do exactly what they want to do all of the time with no consideration for another. These are selfish attitudes which mean, "I am the only one that is important. World, cater to me and make it easy for me to be happy and have everything I want." Psychologically, all of us feel the need for isolation and being catered to from time to time.

Since it is not possible to have a life without conflict, some ministers' wives feel defeated. Seemingly the easiest way to live is to let other people dictate what she should do from hour to hour, instead of being responsible to God for herself. These demands on her life range from the request of a church member for attendance at a meeting to a call to serve as room mother at school to bake cookies for a party. These demands take priority and become the order of the day. Either request should be as just that—only a request. A need has been aired. An opinion has been given. Is it for her? Is that how God would have her invest her time today? What are her priorities? Who is responsible for them?

One minister's wife told me she actually thought that the telephone was God's direction for her life each day. Her priorities were determined by telephone appeals. She could not resist doing whatever was requested of her for the day for fear she might miss an opportunity of service. The philosophy of "being in the right place at the right time or opportunity will pass you by" causes much anxiety to a conscientious Christian. This priority to witness brings confusion to many.

"Joan, come go to a luncheon with us today." Joan's three-year-old has a sore throat and is taking medicine every four hours. Her friend is someone she has been trying to be a witness to. If she doesn't drop all to go, she may feel guilty. She may think she is letting a prime opportunity slip by. If she lets that request become a command for her day at the expense of her child's health, she may be hindering her effectiveness with her friend. Her best opportunity to be a witness just could be her concern for her responsibilities to her sick child.

We become so involved with a general definition of witnessing and trying to be a *superb* example that we easily forget that our life-style is our greatest attraction to someone who is seeking answers in her life. Most experienced mothers would be impressed with a young mother's choice to willingly, with a good attitude, carry out her "mothering" at the expense of a sharing time with other women over lunch.

When the requests of others become priorities, you will experience a remote-controlled kind of living with very little, if any, satisfaction possible. The futility will catch up with you sooner or later. Seek not to be in contact with people who feel they must dictate to you the direction of your life.

A person who is directing her own life needs both short- and long-range plans. She plans by the week, by the month, by the year, and by the overall lifetime where she is going. She needs time to plan, shop, study, build a marriage, enjoy and train children, and carry out work responsibilities. These are daily plans that make up the week. Monthly plans are what make a year go well. The seasons give a variety of emphasis. A very important goal is to stay in charge of your priorities.

What does God want for her? The Scripture instructs her to be sensitive to the needs of those around her. The good Samaritan is an example. He was not going along looking for someone to help; but while he was traveling along he saw a need, realized he could help, and helped. The commission to witness is as the Christian is en route (Matt. 28:19-20). She is to be ready to state the hope that is in her when it is sought (1 Pet. 3:15). She is not to live others' lives. On the contrary, she is to keep God's commandments, accept Christ's love for her, and dispense his love to others as she lives out *her one life.*

We are made by God, created in his image. He does not make us do his will; but he gives us choices throughout our lives. Even Jonah in his rebellion was given choices. He could have gone to Nineveh or stayed in the belly of the fish. A minister's wife can let others dictate her life and be miserable, or she can choose to be in charge of her day and function as she discerns God's will for her.

Individual goals, plans, and schedules are to be made by individuals. Do not allow others to place their standard on you. I do not believe it is possible for a person to be happy or to feel her life is worthwhile if others are allowed to be in charge of her. They cannot be in charge without consent being given. Much of the emotional confusion of our day would be alleviated by our assuming responsibility for ourselves instead of being directed by the whims of others. A minister's wife is a prime target for outside instruction since she is so closely associated with so many people.

One of the ways a minister's wife falls into the pattern of letting others determine her priorities is by falling into the comparison mold. "Our last pastor's wife always planned the church dinners." In other words, "What is wrong with you? Don't you know what your role is?"

Maybe the standard joke that every minister's wife plays the piano or sings is just another way of saying, "Stay in these guidelines." Just because every other minister's wife shops on Tuesday does not mean you must shop on Tuesday unless that fits your schedule.

One of the reasons it is so easy to let others be in charge of your life is that it saves you the time of planning what you are going to do with your time.

Another pitfall for the minister's wife is the use of a general definition for the words evangelism or visitation. This simplified definition can constrict a young Christian woman quickly. While browsing in a bookstore at a retreat, I overheard one young woman asking another if she knew of any books that could help her be a better Christian. As I paused to speak to them, they asked me to recommend a book for them. When I asked, "What area of growth are you interested in?" the reply was, "I just want to bear fruit. I have never won a person to the Lord. I feel so guilty around other Christians. I just never seem to have witnessing opportunities." My next question was, "Do you have children?" One answered, "Yes, three."

Our conversation moved from the bookstore to a shade tree on the lawn. As we continued to share, I thought back to my days with a young family and how inadequate I felt when fruit bearing was mentioned. I shared, "But the fruit of the Spirit is love, joy, peace, patience, kindness, goodness, faithfulness, gentleness, self-control; against such things there is no law" (Gal. 5:22-23, NASB). The state of being who you are, where you are, in relationship to Christ offers exactly what God would have you be today.

Our actions need the foundation of our being. The book of James says that our faith works. If a woman feels crummy about herself, then she makes a crummy impression for Christ. However, a woman who sees herself as being as valuable to God as any other human being has discovered abundant living and is proof to others that her faith works for her.

I do not consider myself to be an excellent gardener, but I do know that a seed must be planted and given time to grow. You cannot plant an apple seed one day and expect to eat apples off of the tree the next day. Digging the seed up to see how it is growing is not a good idea, either. There are stages of growth that are normal, and they take time. The process of growth involves planting a seed in prepared soil, sprouting, leaves, branches, blossoms, time for maturation, and then fruit. All of these stages have to be important in fruit bearing. Maturation is a lifelong process for the wife of a minister also. She needs to use what is there today for growth to take place.

When you decide on the direction of your life, you need to remember that God's input through his Word and by his Spirit is essential. Without it, we grope from day to day with no spiritual growth and limited emotional development. With God's help it is possible to develop an adaptability to handle new or changed circumstances. This kind of flexibility makes a person capable of modification (in charge of herself) and able to bend without breaking. This is a virtue that is worth cultivating. There are opportunities that come, for example, with relocation. If she moves looking at what she will have to work with (the positives) instead of what she is losing (the negatives), the adjustment will come about more quickly.

How a person feels about herself is displayed in her appearance. The posture, the countenance, the style or type of dress all say how she feels today about herself. It is good periodically to linger before the mirror and study your image. I read advice from a beauty consultant with whom I very much agree. She was encouraging women to choose *your* color, *your* dress to fit *you* and your life-style, and to major on what is *right* with *your* figure, and not always to work from a corrective point of view. If you work from a positive point (what is good to me), the areas that you feel are not so good will not be that noticeable to others.

Clothing you feel comfortable in usually is more attractive on you. I am not suggesting blue jeans and a sweatshirt on Sunday morning. There needs to be an appropriateness of dress which is determined by the occasion, where you are going, and what the dress standards are in your community.

The overall outward appearance of a woman gives the first impression of her as a person. Look at what you are trying to say to those around you. The person who is sloppy or disheveled may be trying to call attention to herself more than the person who is neat, clean, precise, and outgoing. Sometimes the message is, "Poor me. I do not have enough money, time, or energy. Don't you feel bad that you (church members) have mistreated me?"

A church member recently commented to me about their youth minister and his wife, "If they were poorly dressed and did not keep their car so washed and polished, people would be willing to pay them more salary." Whether that is true or not, how the couple saw themselves with a small salary shows they cared about managing what they had.

Your body is the temple of God since the Holy Spirit dwells in you (see 1 Cor. 6:19). Your body is your house on this earth. You are the only one responsible for the upkeep and decoration. The care a woman gives to herself to see that health is maintained is a personal trust from God. The rest—food, cleanliness, and overall use of the body—is part of her stewardship to God.

Attractiveness is high on the list of most women in defining femininity. Attractiveness and seductiveness are not the same. The Scripture warns against trying to arouse men sexually to build your self-esteem. An attractive person is one whose overall outward picture makes others want to be near her. They desire the radiance and peace that is displayed by her being happy to be who she is, where she is. Christ is also seen as desirable when those who follow him are attractive.

Have you ever had the privilege of hearing a Christian say, "Follow me and I will show you how to be pleasing to God"? I have only read that in the words of the apostle Paul in 1 Corinthians 4:16; 11:1.

What is wrong with asking someone to follow us? Why are we fearful? Is this not what Jesus taught when he commissioned us as his representatives on this earth? Paul was instructing us to share where we are and to help others to know what Christ is able to do because we have experienced his power in our lives. The crafts teacher is using the "follow me principle" as she shares her skills with others.

A minister's wife does not need to feel that she must have every area of her life fully developed in order to give leadership to another person. We are to share. The requirement for giving is to give what you have. You have something to share that you have found to be true. The people around you have needs that you can meet by being genuine.

Identity is from the *now* perspective. It cannot be found in what you want to become. That is tomorrow. We must begin with who we are *now*. That is *really* who we are. There are some things within the person we are that are lovable and worthwhile just as we are today.

We sometimes get so hung up on the alterations and corrections that we need to make in order to be perfect that we lose sight of what we already have. In a sermon Dr. James Sullivan said, "The oak tree is the perfection of an acorn." Most Christians could benefit greatly by this concept of growth. The minister's wife will miss the joy of entertaining guests if she waits until she can do it well enough to be photographed for *Better Homes and Gardens.*

Have you ever been angry with God because you felt that he did not give you much to work with? We are ashamed or even afraid to admit that we are not always pleased with our lot in life. We go into an explanation to others of how God is in control, that he has placed hardships in our life in order to train us; then subconsciously or privately we examine and reexamine ourselves to see why we deserve such treatment. Let's not discount the world we live in, nor the fact that we are touched by the effect of sin.

Jesus' prayer in John 17 helps us to realize that problems will be with us, but we can overcome them. The evil that creeps into our lives almost unnoticed is discouragement. Vance Havner in his book *Though I Walk Through the Valley* says that "under the circumstances" is no place for a Christian. When problems and circumstances control our thinking, we are destined for despair. God promises to walk with us through the circumstances. We will not necessarily feel good about them, but we can work through whatever the world hands us with Christ's Spirit, strength, wisdom, and peace, knowing he will never leave us or forsake us. When I sat by my husband's bedside for thirty-six days while he was dying, I felt "under the circumstances." By reading Dr. Havner's book I gained encouragement and a new perspective in the midst of my grief. Circumstances can control only when there is human resignation to them.

To the degree that you can learn to like yourself and accept yourself, you can give freedom to others to seek their particular gifts and expressions. You also will have a part of the definition for a minister's wife that will be pleasant to live by.

3
The Child Has Become an Adult

Why is there a need to define "daughter"? It seems that the term daughter is pretty obviously defined. She is a female person born to parents who have named her. A daughter is a daughter — what else?

The reflection of who she is is needed because there are many difficulties in the parent-daughter relationship when, as often happens in our society, the guidelines have not been defined. She is trying to work from three different directions: hers, her mother's, and her father's. Part of the need can be seen in the old saying, "A son is a son until he marries a wife, but a daughter is a daughter all of her life."

The role of the parents is fairly simple to state but very difficult and complicated to perform. Parents are responsible for training each child in the way that is best for the child. Most parents try to give a child the best they have to offer according to their capabilities. A daughter receives from her parents guidelines, or the lack of guidelines, for self-discipline. Her parents have given her a picture of what God is like, how love works, and what a marriage relationship is. They have influenced her value system. Much of what she has built into her was accomplished by seeing, hearing, and experiencing her parent's lives. The objective of every parent should be to take a very dependent child and guide her to become independent.

In a recent survey, parents were asked if they would have children again. One father said, "No, because you spend all of that time raising them and they become independent and don't need you and leave you." How sad that his life was being lived in his children — sad for him because he had neglected his own growth and interests. Sad for the children because they were probably shackled with the false guilt of feeling responsible for their father's unhappiness.

The relationship that a daughter has (in her early years) with her parents is one of admiration and love or distrust and need. At that time, all of life is revolving around the parents' ability to supply what is needed for her. There are two kinds of children—obedient and rebellious. We are sometimes a mixture of both. I often hear a woman say in group situations and in private consultation that they have been the perfect daughter as a child. She always obeyed her parents and never did anything wrong, but now as an adult she feels angry about it.

Recently I asked a woman who expressed these feelings why she resented being a model child. Her reply was, "I realize now that obedience was the price I paid to be loved and am still paying." Her parents are only pleased with her when she is acting as they want her to act. A minister's wife I admire very much was accused by her mother of not being a very good Christian because she would not put her first in her life.

Everyone interprets her parents' actions toward her as she saw them, not necessarily as the parents intended. Sometimes parents are strict with the intention of protecting their children. The child may interpret the parents as rigid or withholding fun. Time seems to blur her memories, and she recalls what she chooses. A few years ago I conducted a three-day seminar in Phoenix, Arizona, where my family all live. I had a rare opportunity of sharing with them. My mother, sister, brother, and I were reminiscing about our childhood. It was a rude awakening to realize how differently each of us remembered the same experiences. Each one was filling in from his own perspective. All views were valid because of the way they were experienced and how they affected us at the time.

Anne Davis shared with a ministers' wives group an experience of misunderstanding between her and her mother in early life that could have been disastrous had they not corrected it. She stated that when she was nine years old, she spent the night with a friend. Her friend's mother tucked them in and kissed them goodnight. Anne said it was a great experience because her mother had never tucked her in and kissed her goodnight. Anne spent much time and energy over the next ten years of her life wondering why her mother did not love her. When she decided to ask her mother why she did not love her, her mother was overwhelmed. She questioned Anne if she had not seen the clean dresses, mended socks, and polished shoes ready for her each morning when she awoke? Anne's mother was saying each day "I love you" with the kind of expression she had missed because of the death of her mother at a very early age.

It is necessary that we share verbally with our children what our expressions of love mean.

The ideal would be for parents to equip each child so that she is capable of independence and self-control when she reaches young adulthood. A minister's wife may feel cheated because she has not been prepared to carry out the responsibility and control for herself.

The relationship to parents of a nine-year-old girl and a thirty-year-old woman would not be the same. However, it is very easy to remain in a small-child category to parents even in adult life if we do not take time to consider what the relationship should be after we are adults. Some parents continue to give instructions to adult children. This advice should be considered as a valuable opinion, not a command. An opinion carries the freedom to be accepted or rejected.

Some women have resentment toward one or both of their parents because of feelings of being denied the right kind of training as a child. I have seen this resentment used as an excuse for various behavior patterns in life. When one says, "I cannot help the way I act, I was raised that way," she is making an excuse for poor behavior instead of being responsible. Our childhood training is what we have to begin working with in our adult life. But it does not mean that we must continue in the same pattern all of our lives unless we choose to do so. Blaming someone else for your present behavior will never correct the behavior or give you the perspective for you to plan your future. No person has had a perfect set of parents. Regardless of what training you have been given, you can use it to your advantage if you will learn from it.

While in a Christian marriage group, Joan said, "My parents did not contribute one positive thing to my life." I told her, "That is hard for me to believe." I suggested life, looks, education, cleanliness. She left the group still feeling very cheated by her alcoholic parents and her unstable homelife. Several months later Joan became involved with a family where real compassion was needed. She shared with me after she had ministered to some of the family members that for the first time, she could see that her empathy had come out of her background.

"And we know that God causes all things to work together for good to those who love God, to those who are called according to His purpose. For whom He foreknew, He also predestined to become conformed to the image of His Son, that He might be the first-born among many brethren" (Rom. 8:28-29, NASB). This Scripture does not say that these things feel good or will be pleasant things. If we seek to mature in our relationship to Christ, we will use everything we have learned to benefit ourselves and those around us.

To love is a charge that is given to all Christians. To love one's parents as a child is usually not that difficult. I have even seen battered children who were willing to return to their parents and give them another chance just because they were their parents.

As adults we are commanded to honor our parents, and this becomes a bit more difficult for some. To *honor* means "to value and give respect" for what they have done. Honoring is after the fact. Those who prefer to look at what was wrong instead of what was right will have a problem honoring their parents. It helps to remember that they gave you life, training to the best of their ability, and love by their definition.

Relating to parents as an adult daughter can be accomplished without too much difficulty when all three agree on the definition and purpose of building a good relationship.

Some daughters have to be literally pushed out of the nest even after marriage. Their desire is to have the best of two worlds. When an adult continues to look to her parents for guidance, security, and approval, she is harming if not hindering the building of a marriage. First loyalties can no longer be given to parents when marriage has been entered into. The Scripture emphatically states four times that there must be leaving of parents and preferring of husband in order for marriage to work (Gen. 2:24; Matt. 19:5; Mark 10:7; Eph. 5:31). Clinging adult daughters could be helped the majority of the time by talking with their parents about the difficulty they are having in leaving. The parents could give the encouragement that is needed for the daughter to be independent.

On the other hand, there is another area of leaving that is not so easily dealt with. Sometimes parents see the daughter as an extension of themselves. They expect their child to share her life with them totally if she wants to be accepted. Many adult daughters are called on to prove their love and appreciation constantly in the manner that is dictated by the parent.

A few years ago a radiant Christian woman, who is a pastor's wife, attended one of my *Woman — Aware and Choosing* classes. She was a very open person and shared her feelings freely. Her relationship with her mother seemed to be the area where she felt she was failing in her Christian life. As we discussed her daughter-mother relationship, Carol realized that each time she did not carry out her mother's wishes, her mother accused her of not being a good Christian. Most of the time she was expected to meet the requests, which were really demands, before consideration of her own children, her husband, or what the Lord had already assigned her for that day.

Carol began devoting her prayer time to seeking solutions instead of asking for patience and begging the Lord to change her mother. She began sharing with her mother her loyalties in the order that she saw them according to God's Word. She learned that saying no to her mother was not a dishonorable act; rather, she was being responsible for her own life. Obedience to God does not free us of the decisions that must be made. Carol set aside a special time each week for her mother, and after a period of adjustment both are enjoying the adult relationship they are building. Just recently Carol said to me, "My relationship with my mother now makes it possible to see so many of her contributions that I had not noticed before and has relieved me of the weight of guilt that I had hanging over me." Carol's dilemma is a very common problem.

Recently at the Southern Baptist Convention I heard the parent-daughter relationship being discussed in three different groups with varying degrees of frustration. The hindrances were unsolvable because they had not built adult-to-adult relationships.

What makes adults run from their parents, resent their parents, or refuse to be involved with their parents? Often the reason is that the parents want to live the adult child's life and not their own. There is no easy way for an adult child to establish an adult relationship with parents who wish to remain in control. But this must be done in order for her to build her own marriage and family. I am not suggesting that a daughter should cut her parents out of her life. In love she needs to share where she is and who she is with her parents.

She is the only one who can give current information to them about herself. They need to understand from her that the marriage relationship requires the giving of first consideration, loyalty, support, and preference to the husband. Father's advice can no longer be measured alongside that of her husband unless her husband chooses to seek that advice. With marriage there are now two different backgrounds to take into consideration. What each marriage partner has been taught is what is comfortable to them.

The traditions of childhood need a contemporary evaluation. Some of our identity and enjoyment goes back to what was established in our childhood home. Most of us try to carry over those *good feelings* by trying to relive those great times. We try to do everything the same way.

Sue, a financially successful woman, sought my help. She felt that her entire world was falling apart. The conflict regarding Christmas was wrecking her holiday. Her husband and three teenage children wanted to fly to a ski resort for the Christmas holidays. Sue would not be able to go through all of the *tradition* they had been carrying on with her parents all their married life. Sue said, "My parents just will not understand." With a great deal of encouragement from me, she decided to tell her parents about her family's change in plans. She encouraged her parents to make plans of their own. Sometimes this sharing gives parents a new freedom in their lives also. They might like to get out of the rut of hanging up the stocking after thirty-five years. Sue's experience caused a new awareness of living for today and not trying to recapture yesterday. Her family is experiencing new sharing from year to year instead of a sameness.

All of us live in some traditional bind if we are not really planning for today. We say, "We have always done it this way, so that is the only valid way." Not so. We change; our needs change; our relationships should change as we mature.

Also, it should be remembered that children are gaining their patterns about how to build an adult relationship with you by watching you with your parents.

Many times parents' love is based on performance. Because of this we grow up with this attitude about God: If I do perfectly, then he loves me.

Performance for acceptance becomes a pattern between the parents and a daughter; this must be consciously altered, or her life is miserable. It is also miserable for the parents because they feel that since the daughter is not performing, she does not love and appreciate them. It is a pressure of guilt to the daughter because she cannot seem to do enough to please the parents. The minister's wife normally lives out of the area where her parents live. Pressures are applied to her when her parents require a letter on a specific day. If the young woman (because of her priorities) cannot possibly write, many parents will punish her by not writing to her. Sometimes the parents will write, scolding the daughter as if she were a child for being selfish or inconsiderate.

In defining daughter, remember that you wear this label because of your parents' lives; but you are the *person* wearing the label. Your definition will involve the person you are, what is important to you, and where you are. A good daughter cannot be defined as one who visits her mother and father each day if she lives three thousand miles from them. She also may not be able to visit them every day if they are very near. A minister's wife needs to decide her priorities to have direction for her life. This prepares her to talk with her parents to tell them where she is and how she feels about herself in relationship to them. These expressions should be done with love and appreciation.

Parents many times seek to have first consideration in their daughter's life, to the detriment of her marriage. When this preference is given (you can tell if it is if what they say to you is given more consideration than what your husband says), it must be stopped. Else a *becoming one* cannot take place in the marriage.

Many young couples experience a great deal of dissension when visiting parents. The greater part of the time this is because of the two loyalties. She is pulled apart. Parents want first consideration. Husband wants first consideration. The child in her says, "I only see my parents once a year, month, or week. We deserve to have this exclusive time without interference." The husband is given the accusing message, "Grow up!" The wife in her says, "Why can't he love my parents and let them be first part of the time?"

In-law problems can only be solved from a parent-child vantage point. A daughter can speak to her parents about the need she has for encouragement in her marriage. However, a son-in-law could ask this same thing of her parents for his wife and be considered an *outsider* who is trying to take her affections from them.

The extension of the daughter label to include daughter-in-law becomes a disappointment for many because they are using the daughter definition. Daughter-in-law is a separate category and must be defined in relation to husband as he relates to his family, not as the woman relates to her family as a daughter. Trying to become a daughter instead of a daughter-in-law is an effort to establish a child instead of an adult relationship. It could only be spelled out by your background, which will call on you to expect his parents to measure up to your parents. This is placing a parent-to-you definition on them that they cannot meet because they do not understand what that was to you. Calling for your husband's response to his parents by your standards is trying to change his relationship with his family. A wife may even nag her husband, trying to get him to relate to his parents by her standard. "Every good son acts this way to his mother on Mother's Day!"

It is an impossible mission for a wife to try to establish a relationship for her husband with his parents when no relationship exists, or to try to change an existing relationship. Relate to your in-laws as the wife of their son. This way you are free to see them from an adult perspective. He knows them and where he is with them, and he makes an excellent guide for you.

When the husband's parents interfere in the marriage, the problem must first be dealt with on a husband-wife level. She should tell him where the difficulty is as she sees it and how it is affecting her. The husband-son must be left free to deal with it in his own time and his own way. Remember, he is sensitive to his parents and aware of his relationship with them.

Competition between a man's mother and his wife is a common problem. Some mothers overemphasize their label and feel it calls for making a son's decisions and even seeing that the adult son carries them out. When this is the case, the mother can become jealous of her son's wife when first place is transferred to her (as it must be in marriage). There cannot be competition without two people involved. When a wife refuses to be a second mother, she is making her own place—not taking another's place. The relationship can only be established if the wife and mother-in-law want it to be.

The older man and woman should be the trailblazers in establishing a good in-law to daughter-in-law relationship. They have experience to build from. They should be the ones to lay the groundwork by announcing what names they want to be called (remembering that adults are involved). They need to state invitations instead of assuming that all details will be carried out as usual. It is helpful to give space and time for newlyweds to establish their marriage and new friendships with input only when asked for.

Part of the definition of the "daughter" label when a woman is married involves moving down in relationship priority. The marriage relationship takes precedence over the parent-child association. This is not easily established. Even a once-a-year visit can show a husband he is not first, and the feeling he has lasts until his wife is with her parents again. For the husband will sense that it is not only for one week that parents are given first consideration; this is true all of the time. First place is first place all of the time, in all relationships, or not first place at all.

When parents are in poor health, the fear of losing them can cause even greater pressure. Several years ago my father was critically ill, and I left my husband and three children and flew to be with him and my mother. Days and nights blended together as we changed shifts at the hospital. I was hardly aware of what day of the week it was. I called my family daily to report on my father and to hear how they were doing without me. After ten days my husband asked me to come home for a few days because of his schedule. Deciding who is the most important person in your life is very difficult in this kind of situation. I went home. My father lived five more weeks. While it was a very difficult decision, I also found it a very rewarding one. Husbands need to know by action that the "wife" label is given first consideration over the "daughter" label.

When and if the time comes that parents are not able to care for themselves and must be cared for, some decisions must be made. It is best if these guidelines can be constituted ahead of time. Paul said to Timothy (1 Tim. 5:8), "But if any one does not provide for his own, and especially for those of his household, he has denied the faith, and is worse than an unbeliever." Verse 16 speaks to the woman as also being responsible for her parents if they are unable to care for their own needs.

A young minister shared with me his feeling that if there was a son in the family, it was his responsibility to care for parents because a son provided the financial income. However, women earn finances too. Are finances the only involvement to be considered in this parent problem? What about the hours of meeting needs? The emotional drain? The husband and wife can partly prepare for this time if it should come for either set of parents. By a marriage decision they can determine what needs the parents have that the two of them can meet.

The parent-child pressure is exerted when the parent communicates the attitude of, "Look at all I have done for you." Or the stress can come from the refusal of the parent to let the daughter/son be a part of the planning by saying, "I am not going to be a burden on my children," yet making no plans.

Many people feel that caring for parents necessitates providing for them in the manner that they dictate. In observing this parent-care situation for thirty years, from many age levels, I have seen that the focus on the parent-child relationship is critical. It seems that the more alienated parents and children are, the more necessary it is to consider every whim as the instruction of the day. "A caring child does not treat a parent this way" is the way guilt is used to control the child. The overall factors such as health, facilities, time, and finances must be taken into consideration as to where the parent will live. The decision should not be made on feelings of the moment or what outsiders think. It is not a one-member decision but a marriage decision, as well as one between all persons involved. The sacrifice of one's health, either physical or emotional, for the aging parent's convenience or wishes, is untenable. Alternate solutions must be found.

It is necessary that communication be kept open between husband and wife. Each one needs to share how he feels honestly and forthrightly. Decisions regarding the parent's care should be made on a trial basis, and honesty is of utmost importance. Remember, first consideration must be given to your mate, not your parents. Many adult children are destroying their lives and their marriages by trying to do everything exactly as the parent demands. These demands are made according to the rules that were established in childhood. "You do not love me unless you perform the way I say, or you are not accepted as a good daughter if you do not perform my way." There is also the pressure of silence—the parents cut off an adult-child to control her.

The provision for parents should be a joint effort of all children. This is more than financial provision. Bitterness results in a family when one child takes on all of the responsibility. It should not be an adults' "catching up" time, but a meeting of the parent's current needs. All of a parent's needs cannot be met by the children. There must be some effort put forth by the parents to be responsible for themselves. If care is in the home, then the parent needs to come under the structure of that particular home as a family member, not as the guide or guest of the household.

Recently a young man shared with me how he had dealt with his mother after his father's death several years ago. He was a young husband and father. He invited his mother, who felt she could not live alone, and his younger brother to live in his home. The conditions were that she must turn her finances and property over to him and move into their home as a family member. He would be the overseer, and her needs would be met. This helpless mother, placing all kinds of guilt on her married son, decided quickly she could stay in her home. She apparently did not want to become a part of a family where she was not to be given first consideration. The relationship was strained for a period of time, but today they are working with an adult definition of son.

The adult-daughter definition needs to take into consideration the present person she is, the commitments she has made, the love that she wishes to express, and the recognition that the principles are to live by. Others may contribute ideas and opinions, but in the final analysis she is responsible to God for herself.

Some helpful guidelines are: (1) Define your adult-daughter responsibilities toward mother and father. (2) List your parent's positive contributions to your life. (This shows where you can honor them.) (3) What do you see as your parent's greatest needs from you at this time? Can you honor these needs and still build your marriage?

One of the greatest struggles in identity begins in the area of defining adult-daughter.

4
Creative Images

"If you wish to break the engagement I will try to understand because you agreed to be my wife when I planned to go into business. Now I have decided I must preach God's word. I hope the change in direction of my life will be acceptable to you because I very much want to marry you." These words came to me in a letter from a young sailor six months after we had become engaged. As a young woman in love I answered, "I do not care what job you have. After all, I agreed to be your wife; and your wife is what I want to be."

A young woman in love rarely thinks of relating to her husband's profession. She is more concerned with being a wife to the man she has chosen to marry.

A wife is a married woman. Is there need to say more? The label "wife" is one in relation to the man with whom she has chosen to become one. For the minister's wife, this label carries a blessing (or burden) of varied interpretations.

Let's consider the choice of the wife label on the basis of qualifications as we would other labels, such as teacher, accountant, or realtor. After much thought and relating to a number of people through the growing-up years, a woman decides she wants to be the wife of the man of her choice. She thinks he will make her life complete and she will be happy.

There are few events that call for as much excitement as a wedding. Everyone gets into the act. From the announcement of engagement until the bride's bouquet is thrown, there is involvement of many interested parties. Much time is spent on the wedding, but very little time is spent in preparation for the marriage. We act as if it is just understood that a woman is to realize what is expected of her as a wife because her mother was a wife.

The minister's wife is handed even more confusion by virtue of her

51

position in the church now. The commitment being made in marriage was indicated when Jesus said, "Have you not read, that He who created them from the beginning made them male and female, and said, 'For this cause a man shall leave his father and mother, and shall cleave to his wife; and the two shall become one flesh'? Consequently they are no more two, but one flesh. What therefore God has joined together, let no man separate" (Matt. 19:4-6, NASB). This commandment is a sensitive point to a minister's wife if she feels this means one person.

Marriage is one of the most significant decisions made in a lifetime. There needs to be thought given to the necessary ingredients to maintain a marriage, to make a marriage survive—more than this, to make the marriage desirable. Being married to a minister does not make an automatic success.

Marriage is somewhat like building a house. Making the plans is exciting. Watching its construction, moving in, and furnishing it are very adventurous steps. As time passes, you add pieces of furniture. One day you become tired of looking at the sameness of it all and start to have a desire for a new house. Some remodeling, painting, planting a new tree, or making a new flower garden can add satisfaction to the house and remove the monotony.

In marriage, the wife steps starry-eyed into a new relationship. In time children are born, and a family relationship begins. Children are not to become part of the marriage. The biblical instruction is that the *two* (husband and wife) become *one* (marriage). The solidarity of marriage makes for a strong basis for family life. Children grow and become independent in a home where there is a growing love relationship between husband and wife. This is accomplished by standing together.

An excellent way to enter into marriage, or to revitalize a good marriage, is to be realistic and take a hard look at the wife's contribution to the relationship. A second look is needed at what is expected by a wife in the way of returns from a husband.

It would do every bride and wife good to make a list of qualifications she could write on an application for the position of wife. I have asked several brides what they thought to be their greatest contribution to the marriage and have had them say, "I am giving myself." If that means that she is a happy, well-adjusted woman, who knows where she is headed in her life—educated, talented, attractive, energetic—who knows what is expected of her under the label wife, she will have very few problems. Many persons have a false idea of marriage. To most, marriage is an idealistic state of magic that causes two people to become what they are *not* because they have found an agreeable person to be their partner. The minister's wife often faces this entrapment by thinking that what she lacks, he will supply.

The term helpmeet is used to describe a wife in a mysteriously spiritual way. Helpmeet to some means that a wife is to help her husband become what God intended him to be. In her mind she is to complete him or make him perfect by her standard. If this is her idea, she immediately sets in to straighten him out. She has a great deal of encouragement from those around her by such statements as, "Behind every successful man is a devoted woman."

I overheard this piece of advice being given to a young minister's wife: "You determine the effectiveness of your husband's ministry." What that young woman heard was, "You are responsible for how your husband relates to God, follows God, relates to people, and leads people." That is not true. Such statements shackle a minister's wife with a burden that is not hers to bear. She does not become responsible for how her husband relates to God or anyone else. She is not responsible for his manners or his thinking. As a wife she is to contribute herself to the building of her marriage. In marriage both persons remain responsible for themselves and become responsible to their mate in the marriage.

One of the most damaging weapons Satan uses on those who really care is to get them to try to live each other's life. When he can accomplish this confusion of identities, we become utterly discouraged. The main reason for this is that you can never have more than momentary success, and you certainly cannot build the marriage by trying to make the other person over.

The futility of trying to live your mate's life for him (and that is what being responsible *for* him means) is sort of like two cars headed down the street in the same direction at thirty miles per hour. Suddenly one driver decides that the other driver is not driving correctly. Without stopping and agreeing to exchange cars, she just steps out to take over for him. Her car crashes because there is no one at the controls. She ends up lying in the street, injured, and the other driver moves right along on his merry way, taking care of his own driving. In some cases he, too, jumps out to take over her driving; and they both crash.

The kind of love that a marriage grows on should not be a sympathetic "Let me show you how to live your life," but rather "I want to contribute to the relationship by sharing myself and doing what I do well and learning more about who you are as a person and where you are going in your life."

A paramount need of a minister's wife is to recognize that being a wife means *relating to a husband*. "Marriage is an intimate personal union to which a man and woman consent, consummated and continuously nourished by sexual intercourse, and perfected in a lifelong partnership of mutual love and commitment. It is also a social institution regulated by the Word of God and by the laws and customs which a society develops to safe-guard its own continuity and welfare" *(Pictorial Bible Dictionary,* Zondervan, p. 511).

We cannot get away from the fact that woman is the completion of the unit of mankind. Woman is the female part; man is the male part. Both are made in the image of God. The two are to become one unit in marriage. All others are outside the marriage. It is an exclusive relationship.

The common definition of a good wife goes something like this: "A female person; responsible for household—which includes cleaning, decorating, and keeping in order; shopping for food and clothing; meals—planning, preparing, serving, and cleaning after; supply adequate support—emotionally for husband and family; be presentable for the particular occasion; in a good mood yet with enough time to do what is needed in the home and out; a provider of part of the family income if needed; and good manager of money." For the minister's wife, add musical, talented in all areas, a gifted teacher, and so on. Sounds more like a Bionic woman to me.

As I tried to be helpful to Bess, a minister's wife in her late thirties, she kept saying, "All I want to be is a good wife." I asked what her definition of wife was and she replied, "All I ever wanted was to be the wife of a happy husband." My response was, "What is that?" She did not know; nor did she have a definition of what a good wife is. There seems to be a great deal of hesitancy among women to feel they have the freedom to define this label. They are looking for their husband to say what he wants from day to day, and they are living in a state of confusion. He is not the wife, so he should not be asked for his opinions until she has decided what she has to offer. Then contribution from the male point of view can be added to how she sees herself.

Add to the above facts that wives have accepted a general definition that has been handed on from one generation to another without individualizing it. There is much misinformation today making a wife responsible for her husband's welfare. Some are saying that a wife is to live for her husband, be responsible for how he feels about himself, make him happy, defer to his every wish, accept his word as truth, allow husband to be God's representative to her. A minister's wife is pressured into this mold by being made to feel that she is rebellious if she does not accept this concept.

There are others who are defining wife in a totally independent way: Do your own thing: live in the same house and share together when it is convenient, *if* it is convenient.

God is not the author of confusion. He established the guidelines for two people living happily together in the marriage relationship in a harmonious way. *Marriage is a time to quit deciding issues with only one opinion.*

In marriage man is assigned leadership. The woman has her own ideas of how leading should be done. The woman was assigned a followship (submission) role, and in some marriages the man feels he is responsible to see to it that she submits. Around and around they go, trying to find new ways to work on their mate's side of the marriage.

The equal partner plan seems to be the most popular alternative in Christian circles. It goes something like this: when man has more knowledge and expertise, he leads; when woman has more knowledge and expertise, she leads. The problem comes when the man thinks he knows best and the woman thinks she knows best. Who decides? The stronger one of the two, the judge, or God's Word? The minister's wife usually sees her responsibility as the one who gives in or gives up for the sake of peace.

Since I am writing to women I will not discuss all that the leadership role entails; but if you are interested, I will recommend the book *Man: Responsible and Caring* (Broadman) by Harold H. Coble, my late husband.

In my opinion there are three choices of how you look at the word submission.

The *passive* definition of submission is an "I don't care. I have no opinion that I wish to share with you." This is silent treatment which is cruel as well as destructive. It is a doormat type of existence that a woman chooses. Basically she is saying, "I will not share myself in this marriage. You never listen anyway." Of course, this wife is very self-serving in her own eyes. She is taken advantage of because she invites that kind of treatment. A wife can only become a doormat if she lies down and invites her husband and family to walk on her. She usually is looking to her husband or others to say how valuable she is instead of recognizing her own worth.

Ron, a husband and father of three small children, said to his wife, "I am leaving because you do not want to work on our marriage." His wife was brokenhearted as she recounted how she kept a neat house, always had his meals ready even though he had a difficult work schedule, and took good care of the children. Ron said, "But in seven years of marriage you have neither participated with me in making decisions nor been involved as a person." She had been taught that a good wife just keeps everything running smoothly, is always there, and agrees with her husband. Passive submission means no personal involvement.

Then there is *pretended* submission. This type of person yields to domination willingly in the name of the Lord. Her attitude often sounds like this: "Husband knows best. Husband is always right. Man is superior. God gives man all of the insight. God holds husband responsible for the wife." This self-righteous person feels that the Lord will protect her just for following, even if she goes against this written Word. She refers to Sarah in the Old Testament as her example of an obedient wife. Even though Abraham tried to pass Sarah off as his sister instead of his wife, Sarah went along with the deception (see Gen. 20:5). This is not a complete picture of Sarah, and she should be remembered by the references made to her in the New Testament:

She was able to conceive because "she considered Him (God) faithful who had promised" (Heb. 11:11, NASB). Also in 1 Peter 3:6 she is mentioned as calling Abraham lord (leader), not brother.

Another woman in the New Testament, Sapphira, shows us how dangerous it is to agree with a husband such as Ananias when doing so means being dishonest with God. Both were struck dead (see Acts 5:1-11).

God's assignment is for husband and wife to become one unit in marriage. A wife cannot bypass her husband and work out her marriage relationship with the Lord. Pretended submission will not last a lifetime. It eventually wears the person down to a no feeling, no caring level. It is a waste of life. God wants the woman as the wife to be a contributor in the marriage to the man who is the husband.

The submission called for in the Bible is one that *participates by sharing*, giving current accurate information about who she is, what she feels about herself and her life situation, what personal goals she has and how she is going about achieving them, what her needs are as she sees them, and what her ideas and opinions are. This information is given to *her husband*. To give something to another, we must let go of it. With her information the husband now has a male point of view and a female point of view. Most decisions in a marriage are reached by agreement. When there is disagreement, marriage reaches a stalemate. The husband's God-given assignment is to make the final decision, which becomes the marriage decision. It is a joint decision because both have contributed to it. For the marriage to work, both must continue to support the decision and work together. The biggest problem for the minister's wife is getting the information about herself ready to submit.

Communication is the tool that is used to submit the information that must be given to another if there is to be a relationship built. Submission is more than communication. It does not just mean to tell and to listen, but also to agree to work together on the goal of marriage (two becoming one). She must let go of the information and support the decision when it is made.

There is a temptation to revert to *pretended submission* when the information is submitted to her husband and he chooses to go against her input. This is where the value of the relationship is evident. If she is doing her part, she will support the final decision.

Pressures from within marriage hurt most. Families are falling apart because marriage is falling apart. This is no less true for the minister's family. Perhaps it is more true due to the nature of unique pressures of the ministry. Families cannot be what we want them to be without a strong marriage base. One point of view is lacking in a broken relationship when a husband and wife are not sharing with each other. This is true even if they still reside in the same house. The broken relationship of husband and wife causes loneliness for both. There is coldness in the home and less effectiveness in the church.

The Research Services Department of the Sunday School Board of the Southern Baptist Convention made a survey of three hundred ministers' wives. The survey had a cross-section of different sizes of churches, varied locations, and wide range of groups. It revealed that the majority of wives have formal education beyond the high-school level. They found being a pastor's wife satisfying and fulfilling, have insufficient income for family needs, and see themselves as Christians with the same responsibilities as any other Christian. They listed their three main pressures: (1) not enough time for self and family; (2) few close friends; (3) inadequate finances. Although they saw themselves with the same responsibilities as any other Christian, there was a contradiction when they came to say where they were in actual involvement. The greater part saw themselves as very involved in their husband's ministry as a team member, but some preferred to be a background supporter.

The pressures that come from within the marriage relationship are not expressed so readily. The grievances are sometimes voiced about the circumstances and not the real difficulty between husband and wife.

There is the problem of time or lack of time. We probably need more help to be good stewards with our time than with our money. Since time is so elusive and cannot be stored, we feel the desperate necessity of cramming it full of activity. There are so many things that we want to do or feel we need to do.

The time factor seems to be a big issue in the life of a minister's wife. To some, it is a problem of her husband being absent from the home so many hours each day. To others, it is having him in the

home to study or home for lunch each day. The fluctuation of schedules causes stress for some wives.

The solution begins with the honest consideration of what kind of
a life she actually wants. For the wife who has a husband who works
from the home base, there is a greater need to organize her own
schedule. An agenda for the day will help her recognize what she has
accomplished. Working out her own timetable helps her feel good
because she has carried out her responsibilities. Indefiniteness robs
her of accomplishment. She is secretly blaming him for the fact that
she does not know what she is going to do next. The resentment she
can store can be directed both at him and at the ministry.

Sometimes a husband will want his wife to sit and talk with him
when they are in the home. Many times he does not have anyone to
share with as a friend. This is an area that needs to be worked
through. One word of warning: If a wife resents leaving what she has
planned to do in order to listen and share with her husband, she
needs to take a look at what she wants to accomplish with her time.
Problems will be minimized when a person has priorities straight; the
husband's needs are more important than dusting a table.

It is imperative to have plans for the day to be able to accomplish a
wife's goals. The husband needs time with his wife. The need is
stated. There could be a regular coffee break time established and
anticipated. If it is to be a "drop in when you feel like it" routine,
then the wife needs to state what time would be easier for her. She
can learn to be disciplined enough to stop for a period of time, then
resume with her routine. Unexpected breaks can be like mini-vaca-
tions. They are refreshing.

If you have a problem scheduling your time as a wife, let me suggest that you do yourself a favor and write down the main things you
want to accomplish in the next seven-day period. Now divide these
tasks into days. Are you being realistic or are you counting on outside
help?

What do you and your husband do with the time you have together? There is the wife that rarely sees her husband and has little
opportunity to share with him. How much time does a couple need in
order to feel they have had adequate time to share? This will vary but
needs to be defined. The loneliness experienced in marriage can be

alleviated by each sharing with the other about themselves. Do you know who you are today? What do you need to bring him up-to-date on about yourself and where you are in your life? Is there a special time set aside where you can give him your complete attention? Do you have construction of the relationship in mind? Are you bringing new information or just wanting to rehash something that has not been decided to your satisfaction?

The length of time we spend together is not the most important factor in building a fulfilling marriage relationship. What we do with the time we have together is crucial. Marriages under the pressures of ministry need special blocks of time away from routine to ensure growth.

You do need time alone. There is the pressure of study time, his and hers. Sometimes a wife becomes so concerned about whether her husband is studying too much or too little and how he is carrying out his responsibilities that she forgets that is not where she needs to be working. Her time alone should be the task she is working on. It is very important that she have some time alone for quiet time and study. Regardless of how much she may spend with the church members, the children, or the husband, she must *take time for herself*. She is in charge of her time and responsible to God for her relationship to him.

I can just hear some wives of ministers saying to God at the judgment, "But, God, it was so important that I listen to others. I thought that was my first assignment." We are not equipped to minister to others until we have related to God ourselves. Let your husband schedule his own time, and you be responsible for your time. This keeps a wife from being a hearsay believer.

Tapes and books are helpful, but what is needed more than anything else is a time with God's Word that will give him an opportunity to meet your spiritual needs. In this way you will have something to share with those around you. There probably is not a more desperate feeling than that of trying to serve out of an empty life. It is like trying to fill another cup from an empty cup: impossible.

What will others think if we insist on time together? Trying to live up to what one assumes others are expecting of a minister's wife is a guessing game that keeps life edgy. One answer to the distasteful living in a glass house is for husband and wife to decide when the drapes are to be drawn. There is privacy for those who wish it enough to draw the line of how much of their lives they are to share with others. God does not hold us accountable for what others think we should be or do. A husband and a wife together can determine a satisfactory amount of time to be together if both share their needs openly with each other. There is a time to be alone and a time to share with others.

Sometimes the marriage relationship is not what you want. Becoming one unit is a growing endeavor. There are adjustments to be made and answers to be found in every marriage. In this area a minister's wife cannot expect the marriage relation to be the entire responsibility of her husband, since he is the leader and since he counsels others. He can read answers out of books and see how they should be in others' lives, but he cannot work out the marriage by himself. He must have the contribution from the wife.

It is more difficult for some than others to work at a maturing marriage. It often seems from a distance that other couples have a good marriage. If that is the case, be assured that specific time together working on their relationship has been spent. A newspaper story told of a man who retired and decided to live in a lighthouse all alone. When asked why he said, "I have run out of cope." Most of us can identify with his feelings. Coping with the growth of a marriage must have outside input from time to time to be healthy.

There may have been a time when marriage worked itself out and both persons in it had their needs met as God intended, but I doubt it. God wants us to share what we have learned with one another and grow as we go. When this is not done and problems develop, a wise Christian seeks the help of a qualified Christian counselor to work through the dilemma.

Divorce is shocking in a minister's home but is highly probable for those who do not face marriage in a realistic manner. We need to decide where each person wants to go in the marriage and set up some plans to get there. In our complex society the togetherness of direction in marriage is needed even more than when the opportunities were very limited and patterns set by the community. The statistics on divorce among ministers and their wives are alarming. The findings contained in a 225-page report, *Pastors in Crisis,* made by the American Lutheran Church, reports: "Serious marital conflict, often with divorce as a potential way out, was cited by twenty-five per cent of the clergy as their major problem and by forty-five per cent of the spouses."

Many ministers and their wives are living in a broken relationship or have failed in building a marriage, thinking that serving the Lord in the church was a substitute.

A minister's wife said to me, "You just don't know my husband." I asked her, "Do *you* know him?" It is one thing to get acquainted with a husband and another to assume she knows him from past information and performance. It is difficult to be faithful to a person whom you do not know. Fidelity or loyalty is an expression of love. Fidelity is a lifetime commitment to marriage, not a day-to-day choice. However, it is carried out on a day-to-day basis. Problems and hurt feelings are bound to happen when two people are trying to move together in the same direction. It helps to work through these times by coming back to define, in his or her judgment, what each is responsible for in the marriage. There is no way to build a marriage without guidelines because they are necessary for opportunity to grow and change.

There is a need to define the husband's role outside of his career. Many women have a very unrealistic idea of how a husband is to function and who he is to be. Expectations come from her father, brothers, and other acquaintances. Many times the wife's idea of husband is like a smorgasbord—a little bit of this, a little bit of that. Her composite forms the fantasy of a perfect husband. There is no such person.

When a couple in the ministry say they have never had a problem in their marriage, they are saying one of several things: they have not had a problem that they could not resolve together; or they have covered their problems with work or duty, or have accepted an unsatisfactory relationship that does not meet their needs.

Some couples give up and live a life of solitude in marriage without even trying to find answers. There are more avenues to seek help and counsel being offered. To confide in a pastor-friend that help is needed is an excellent beginning. When seeking answers, always look for help from your perspective. Sometimes all that is needed is another point of view.

If he cannot help and you are in a remote area where counseling seems impossible, you could write a letter to a Christian counselor, to authors of books that you have read, or to a pastor in another area whom you respect. You may select a counselor by listening to people who have found help in their marriage. Most directors of missions, if they have been in the area long, can give you names of recommended counselors. There are family counseling centers in most cities. The Rosemead Christian Foundation, Box 5000, Rosemead, California 91770 has programs across the country especially designed to help ministers and their wives. This is an excellent program and can be of help to any couple. It is for strengthening marriage. Every marriage needs periodic checkups.

To be effective we must have a strong marriage base. We do not hesitate to seek help in any area of our life that will make us more sufficient in the Lord's service except when we have needs in marriage. We tend to act as if there is something wrong with us if we solicit counsel.

A bed of roses is what we all would like to have because of the fragrance and beauty, but a rose garden must be cared for constantly in order to produce the prize blossoms. There is care of soil, insects to be dealt with, and thorns to be watched for if there is enjoyment to be received. A good marriage also requires consistent effort.

Pressures in a marriage begin to mount when a husband feels that someone or something is more important to his wife than he is. When her first consideration is given to service outside the marriage, there is a breach in the relationship. All of us have known women who have had a burden for the world who have let their own marriage relationship from a wife's standpoint deteriorate. To build a solid, growing marriage relationship, both husband and wife must give first priority to the other.

The little things, like whether it is economical to squeeze the toothpaste down to the last brushing, may be eating at the union all of the time. Is it more valuable to save five cents a week and burn yourself out emotionally or think on more important things? "It's the principle of the thing," I hear someone say. What principle is that—the one that says divide and conquer?

A wife bogged down with many small grievances should see them as warning signs of being discontent with her husband the way he is. She needs to ask herself why she has a need to change him. This can be a mark of poor self-esteem. Robert West has said, "Nothing is easier than fault-finding: no talent, no self-denial, no brains, no character are required to set up in the grumbling business." A poor self-image causes us to criticize others. We do it well because we practice on ourselves. Most minister's wives expect perfection from themselves, whether in child care or Bible teaching. When they fail to reach 100 percent, criticism results.

Anger and old resentments make their demands on us. Anger is a feeling of displeasure resulting from injury, mistreatment, or opposition. It is the strongest of all passions.

Anger can be a healthy part of every life. To live is to feel displeasure from time to time. In marriage it probably comes along more often from opposition or feeling mistreated. The Christian teaching is that we must be in control of our anger at all times. This has been interpreted many times as *not* showing anger. It means to many that when you are offended, act as if it does not hurt and you will be doing a noble thing. Suppress your feelings; or better still, deny your anger; and you are a good Christian. We even make our children say they are sorry, whether they are or not. A typical conversation might go like this:

Mother: "Tell your brother you are sorry you hit him."

Child: "But I'm not sorry." *(She hits him again.)*

Mother: "Yes, you are; and you tell him right now. Be a good girl."

Child: "I'm sorry."

This is done to get the approval of her mother. Mother has started the process of covering up true feelings with right actions and words.

Anger has a progression. Anger is a normal human emotion. However, we are liable for what we do with our anger. The choice (for us) comes in deciding how we will handle anger. When anger comes, we become responsible for what we do with it in relationship to others.

This does away with making others responsible to us, to not displease us, so we will not need to deal with anger.

The second stage of anger is feeling contempt for another. It is a feeling that the person toward whom the anger is directed is empty-headed or without much intelligence. This is a thinking stage of anger and a serious offense. If it is thought and not dealt with, it moves into stage 3.

The third stage is that of verbal outrage resulting from a loss of self-control, accusing the person of being a godless, moral reprobate. This is an attack on the person's being and character. Jesus said a person this angry is attacking one of God's own creation and must answer to him (see Matt. 5:22). We have all experienced the displeasure, the mental accusations, and coming to the place where it exploded on us.

Anger destroys the one who holds onto it. When we are angry, we need to deal with it within the framework of a day. Anger which is not dealt with turns to deeper problems and is stored away to become bitterness, wrath, clamor, slander, and malice. When we fail to control our anger, Paul said, we grieve the Holy Spirit. He cannot have freedom in our life in that particular area if we have anger stored there. Anger hinders relating to the person who has displeased us. Resentment fills that place. If a minister's wife holds onto enough anger, there will come a time when she is unable to have close contact with anyone.

The beginning place to deal with anger is where we run into it most often—self-anger. We are critical and angry with ourselves because we do not perform to perfection. God gives us time to grow. We need to give ourselves time to grow. Somehow because a person is the wife of a minister, she lets others convince her she should have already fully matured emotionally, even though she may only be thirty.

God offers his forgiveness to us when we miss the mark. To accept his forgiveness intellectually is not enough unless we forgive ourselves and receive the cleansing he offers. Errors forgiven should not occupy the thinking of the forgiven one again. This is a matter of choice, since thoughts can be controlled by the individual. We do not have to continue recalling mistakes when we have asked for forgiveness. Use your energy to move on in your life. (Study Eph. 4:26-32.)

Let me share one of my favorite and most-used recipes with you. It is called *How to Deal with Your Anger.*

1. Be in control of yourself at all times.
2. Do not try to control the other person.
3. Do not assume you know how he feels and thinks. Find out.
4. Judge your anger.
   - Are you angry at yourself because you are not perfect again?
   - Are you just in the thinking stage? If so, you can work on through it between you and God.
   - If it has become verbal, ask God for wisdom in dealing with it.
5. Seek forgiveness for what you have done.
6. Be willing to forgive.

Do not ignore the situation, hoping and praying that it will go away. Become involved and settle your differences. Asking God to forgive you for pulling away from your husband when you are angry does not restore the relationship with your husband. Your husband must be asked to forgive so he can also choose to move back into the relationship.

Forgiveness is the remedy for restoring relationships in Scripture. To have fellowship with God, we must confess where we are wrong and that God is right. Confession also calls for agreeing to go his way. He forgives and cleanses us (1 John 1:9). Real restoration of husband-and-wife relationship is brought about by forgiveness. Remember that Christ did not forgive us because we deserve it but because we ask him to, and he loves us. Immediately the thought races through a wife's mind, "I would be willing to forgive if my husband would only ask." And I hear God's Word say, "Forgive us our debts, as we also have forgiven our debtors" (Matt. 6:12, NASB). Whether they deserve it or ask for it—by choice because you value the marriage—forgive.

Forgiveness has two steps. It is an act and a process. The action is to *decide you will forgive.* The process involves following through and *refusing to dwell on the offense.* We need to keep our marriage relationship up-to-date and not rehash each grievance over and over.

Ann is a prime example of what unforgiveness will do to a marriage. After nineteen years of marriage she said, "My husband and I end each 'discussion' by going back to the day of our wedding, when there had been a disagreement over one of the songs to be sung." One of the reasons husband and wife find it almost impossible to stay on a subject and find an acceptable solution is all the backlog of stored anger.

The two competitive areas in the marriage are the ones for the leadership position and proof that there are only two people in the relationship. These are expressed in all of the main interests of both lives.

The enthusiasm and excitement of a young minister after completing his education and getting into his first place of full-time service almost overshadows all else. Married couples in college and seminary all have had the challenge of survival and a common goal—to get out of school alive and well. It seems forever. Sometimes a minister's wife has sacrificed completing her degree. There were not enough finances for two in school, or there were children needing care. Some do not see the need. She may have finished her degree requirements under great stress. Education for two is never easy. Her husband's goal was to complete his education so he could serve.

A wife's goal many times has been to finish so they could get established so life could be normal. Her idea of normal involves many factors. Sometimes it is to be finished with the long hours of study and have time for them to be together, better housing, more security. They are stepping into a new world. Making the transition from classroom to church field takes a planned effort by both husband and wife. When one goal has been accomplished, another needs to be set. Completing your education is not the sum total of life. Two people prepared to launch out need to decide where they plan to go.

The church may become the husband's first love. Many young wives of ministers have been advised that that is the way it should be. Some withdraw and feel left out. Some feel guilty because they are unhappy with playing second fiddle to the church and try to comfort themselves with the idea that this is their contribution to the Lord. This helps for a while. Eventually she realizes there is no serving the Lord by proxy.

Other wives move right in and become deeply involved with

church activities, too. They work beside their husband, doing God's work, but leave the building of the marriage to happen by chance. Schedules get to a hectic pace, tension builds, and there is always something more to do. The emotional health of many ministers' wives shows that this as a lifetime pattern ends in a broken person.

Some wives have planned and trained to have careers outside the home. When this is the case there needs to be agreement about what each is to contribute to and expect from the other.

When there is a working relationship with current accurate information being given to each other, a husband and wife will have something special to give to others.

The becoming one in the marriage means a loyalty to one another that is not given to another person. The first consideration is to your mate's needs above all others, even the most demanding member of the congregation.

Family life is sometimes in competition with marriage. Children are not a part of the marriage. There are *two people only in a marriage.* The competition of a parent for equal time along with the children places the adult in a juvenile position. Sometimes because of his position in the family as the leader and his standing in the community, ministers spend more time as fathers than they do as husbands. Children can cause a break in the marriage if they are allowed to have first consideration with either parent.

In-laws can be a battleground for most couples also. In a marriage class I was conducting several years ago a couple married twelve years sighed, "This is one area where we have absolutely no problem. We will not have homework to do this week." The following week they returned to class looking very depressed. When I asked what was wrong they started to speak simultaneously: "We had not realized how many of our problems are involved with in-laws. Neither of us feel first with the other. We found each feels the other's parents are given more consideration than we are." The competition with in-laws was faced. They began to make plans toward a long-term goal of making each other number one so the marriage relationship could begin to grow.

Outside interests, hobbies, and friends all compete for first place. There is golfing, fishing, gardening, boating, tennis, baseball, or almost any hobby you can name. Every person has a right to relaxation and time to do whatever he chooses—right? Right. We reason that outside interests make us better persons, and that is true if there is time left to share that better person with your spouse. Constant outside interest can mean a rejection of a spouse. This can be remedied by doing a time inventory. Where is the most free time spent—with spouse or hobbies? The ministering couple needs to plan the recreation time carefully. In addition, if a wife feels rejected, she must communicate this to her husband as information he needs. Before she feels left out, she should be sure that she is available to spend special time with him when he is free.

In some ministries, there is such a close working together in the daily schedules that it may or may not be good to have all of your free time together. This would totally depend on the persons and the area in which they live. If free time depends on getting out of town, at least that time must be coordinated.

Where does all of the money go? One of the major problem areas in the life of a wife married to a minister is finances. Plain and simple, there is not enough. Church finance committees should be more aware of the minister's financial needs. Let me suggest some things that can be done to deal with some of the stress of living on a low income.

Ministers and their wives probably do more with the amount of money they have than any other group. This can be accomplished if they work together with a good attitude about finances. The conflict for place of leadership becomes evident in the constant squabble about money.

A survey by a national woman's magazine asked women, "What do you need to feel secure?" These women from a wide variety of backgrounds answered, "Money." Security meant the certainty of enough money to take care of personal and family needs.

Security is very important to every wife. The handling of finances is a part of the relationship that exposes our values and our worth to one another. Some husbands understand the leadership role to mean strictly "I'm in charge of the money with no static from the wife." Others sometimes dump the whole financial burden on her while they supposedly do more important things. The marriage is two, remember? It takes both functioning together to make any amount of money work.

Many times a wife of a minister feels she is as actively involved in the church as he and should be able to say the salary is half hers. Since, in most instances, there is not much money to begin with, if it is divided in half there is sure to be a seesaw battle going on in the marriage. Some women think they can solve the problem by going to work outside the home so each one will have their own money. The attitude needed is not half mine, half yours, but all *ours.*

What will money buy that is worth divisiveness in your life? Will it buy a good marriage, a healthy body, happiness, a right relationship with God, disciplined children? The amount of money is not the problem. The plan of how to spend the money is a problem.

Make a budget. A simple plan can make for efficient money management and matrimonial harmony. To decide together an equitable distribution of finances will keep down a lot of secret manipulation. Since we enter marriage as two independent individuals planning only for one, it is difficult to switch to consideration of another's needs, wants, and desires. Many persons harbor that secret dream of buying a new bedspread when they have a few extra dollars; and before she gets it done it goes for his secret dream, a fishing tackle box or some other hobby material. Resentment builds. Maybe a few choice words are expressed. After this happens several times in the marriage, a competition set in with an edge of bitterness — each spouse trying to outmaneuver the other.

The goal may be to stay solvent or close to it. A goal without a plan (budget) is a dream. A plan must include steps of how you are going to reach the goal and when. Each marriage partner should have a part in the plan and a part of the responsibility. The wife who assumes no responsibility may tend to feel less valuable. If she does not earn dollars she looks at the world's standard (dollars show worth) and becomes dissatisfied with herself. The wife who works outside the home may feel she should be in charge because she earns too. In some cases she earns more than the husband. The wife who is given all of the responsibility of management of the finances is imposed on. You can tell who is in charge of the money by the one who is always saying, "We cannot afford to . . ."

Greed is not something that applies only to those who are financially successful. It is in process when one wants more than he has to the point of being so dissatisfied that he does not work well with what he does have.

I'm constantly amazed at what a couple can accomplish with what they have when they work together and do not use finances to prove who is leader or who is most important.

God's promises to provide for his children are for the minister and his wife too. This just takes a bit more planning.

The physical union of sexual intercourse is meant to be an intimate sharing of two people in marriage. Using the earlier definition of marriage in this chapter, this sexual relationship is to be a nourishing time or building of closeness. This takes time. Time together— building of appreciation for and desire to please each other. A lover thinks about the one loved. There is a desire to be together. There is a sharing by just being together. There needs to be a looking forward to the time when the two can be alone. Even spontaneous times must be looked for, or they will pass right by while her mind is wondering, "What will the neighbors or church members think if I draw my drapes at this time of day?"

Our permissive society places much pressure on us to take lightly the sharing of our bodies with another person. The Scripture is explicit about purity before marriage and our bodies belonging to each other sexually in marriage. There is a lot of sex instruction being handed out in bulk today but very little positive sex education.

A Scripture study by both husband and wife, using Dr. Herbert J. Miles, *Sexual Happiness in Marriage,* as a guide would be a profitable time spent. The special study would provide opportunities for discussing the hang-ups that both partners brought to the marriage. What is needed more than anything else is firsthand information that is gathered in a relaxed, intimate atmosphere.

When published materials portray every woman acting a certain way or every man thinking a certain way, it is unreliable information. In *Made for Each Other* Dr. John Drakeford discusses the danger of operating in marriage on inaccurate information. Each person has a need to express what is satisfying and enjoyable to him regardless of what might have been stated by someone else.

The sexual information both husband and wife have brought to the marriage from their separate backgrounds can cause difficulty. We've observed the way our parents have treated each other and the value they placed or failed to place on their own marriage. The love expressions between them have influenced what seems right or wrong for marriage. Coming with two sets of rules or standards—one from the husband and one from the wife—calls for a sorting through in order to decide what is right for this marriage.

There is a command given from God in this area in 1 Corinthians 7. After we have chosen to marry, we are no longer to live separately. The sexual desires of the woman are to be met by her husband, and his sexual needs are to be met by his wife. This does not mean only the physical aspect of sexual activities but a total loving sexual relationship. Emotional needs are to be met as well as physical needs. Some of the needs that should be discussed are those of sharing, intimacy, approval, appreciation, alone times, and the point of view of each other for perspective. Marriage is a creative project that takes a lifetime of involvement to define from the female and male experience. It takes time and interest in the other person to build a marriage.

To deprive one another sexually is to rob one of the ingredients due him in marriage. Prayer is specifically mentioned as one thing that is not to be used as an excuse for not sexually sharing together. I'm not sure but that Paul put this in for ministers and their wives because of their busy schedules. Prayer is vital to our spiritual relationship with God and is something that we tend to have a difficult time finding room for in our busy lives. By mentioning prayer, is God not saying that we will have to make a conscious effort not to neglect one another in marriage?

God created us male and female to love, nourish, relate to, share with, and meet the needs of each other. The meeting of each other's sexual needs is given as a way of overcoming temptation in this area of life. Ministers and their wives are not exempt from sexual temptation, especially when their needs are not met. The way of escape that God has provided for sexual temptation is the fulfillment of needs by a wife and a husband.

Our society seems to be obsessed with mass sexual stimulation. We have lost our sense of decency in many areas. The devil is suggesting to the modern Eve, as he did the first Eve, that God's rules for enjoyment and fulfillment for her needs are cheating her of pleasure. Satan has taken the beautiful sex union God created for marriage and has displayed it outside of marriage—full view—wide screen. Because of the wrong use of sex, many wives label sex as wrong. They have failed to differentiate between proper and improper sexual behavior.

Sex out of context is wrong and destroys lives. We can fall into the trap easily because of constant pressure. Because of the fast pace of change in our society, it is amazing how right wrong seems sometimes. We are indoctrinated from day to day to believe there are no faithful people left. We may feel that everyone deserves to be happy and loved without question. If marriage is not automatically satisfying, the world tells us it must be wrong.

There is such a premium placed on having everything our heart desires. We are bombarded through the media. There is a strong emphasis on having what you want now and being happy regardless of what it may cost others. Our motto today, according to the media, could well be—we deserve to be happy, especially sexually happy.

Adultery is not a one-step sin. It begins with entertaining the thought that someone besides your husband could make you happy. A good-looking man walks onto the stage of your life. You begin to fantasize—desire grows and temptation mounts. He looks good. You reason that he could make you happy. You say in essence, "You are right, Satan—God's Word is too strict. I deserve . . ."

With every temptation God has provided a way of escape (1 Cor. 10:13). Marriage is God's answer. The same amount of positive thought given to a husband, the same amount of time given in preparation for your time with him, the same amount of effort to share yourself would result in a good marriage, not a broken one or a boring one. The happy wife is one who is responsible for her own happiness and not looking for it in others. A husband cannot bring happiness to a wife who has decided she wants to be miserable.

It is important that we maintain our feminine identity. In a group of Christian young women I proposed the question, "What is femininity to you?" There was an explosion of rebellion to the word. The main objection was to being classified as a helpless, frilly, doll-type woman. Feminine simply means female—what God created. Feminine identity means your identity as a woman. To try to be the same as the man or like the man means giving up your identity for his. Each woman must decide for herself what it means to be a female. The distinction needs to be clear in her own mind and shared with her husband. I am in no way suggesting that a wife is to become a game player in her marriage. The ideas that she is responsible for making her husband feel happy, for giving him self-esteem, and for making him successful are impossibilities. These are all personal accomplishments, not contributions from the wife. As a wife she should want to be a happy person who affects and encourages him. She should recognize his accomplishments, but she is *not responsible for how he lives his life.*

A woman's attitude about herself will indicate how much she is willing to participate in the process of making their sexual experiences meaningful. A woman's used feeling comes from a negative attitude about herself and naturally about him. Using sex as a method to get what she wants or to make her husband feel inadequate are dangerous emotional games. To make the sex act a test of one's love is defining love in a limited way and basing needs on strictly a physical level.

Even in our Christian walk we base love on how we feel too much of the time. To structure life on feelings only is to miss three-fourths of life. We are mental, physical, spiritual, and emotional beings. When circumstances hand us a day of frustration and Mrs. Irritation has been on our back all day, we have the choices of taking it out on our husbands by telling him all of the gory details, being stone cold all evening as if he were not there, or relating to him. Being responsible for ourselves and not surrendering to Mrs. Irritation shows real love. We need to realize that we are in control of ourselves. Differences can only be worked out with the person with whom we have the difference.

Because of the media's emphasis, some men are overstimulated sexually by viewing half-nude women; the availability of sex has made many husbands less able to perform sexually with their wives. It is also injuring many women because they feel they must compete with other women to allure their own husband. The constancy of problems in other people's marriages and problems ever-present in the church families make it difficult to shift gears from ministering to others to sharing physically and emotionally with each other. Some wives have complaints that everyone else's needs are met before theirs are even acknowledged. This is where the game begins to be played, "If you don't hear me I will not listen to you"; and communication lines deteriorate.

One minister's wife said to me, "I have felt this a thousand times, but when I would share it my husband felt threatened and became defensive. He would tell me he expected more of me spiritually and emotionally." This wife learned to share specific areas where she was hurting and offered time for remedying the situation.

Who's to say when there is too much or too little sex? There is no place for outsiders to decide what the needs are inside the marriage. We do not need to try to live up to some national average. The wife needs to participate in the relationship contributing her total self to add to the union from her side of the bed. She must learn to enjoy giving and receiving. Mainly she must accept responsibility for becoming involved.

Communication is a necessity. How can two persons walk together unless they agree where, how, and when they are going? Communication is the vehicle that is used to gather the information so that there might be agreement. A minister's wife who shares about herself as she finds new information is giving to the marriage. As she listens she is gathering information about her husband and how he is changing. This is vital information for both. Occasionally I hear a passing comment that one person in a marriage has outgrown the other. I always think how sad that is when they have had the opportunity to grow along together, but they have withheld information from one another. Withholding about oneself will cause loneliness, aimlessness, and separateness. Husbands and wives are supposed to be the best of friends, yet she does not withhold information about herself from a good friend. Why the fear? Rejection in the past, not liking herself, or not caring enough about him?

To communicate is to tell your husband about yourself and to listen to what he tells you about himself. To have communication there must be a sender and a receiver, and each must function in both positions.

Too much of the time a minister and his wife do their communicating about the schedules of the day, what time the next meeting will be, what messages she has received by phone or by visit, the complaints, illnesses, deaths, and what is wrong with the kids, the washer, or the dog. Her frustration and lack of value as a wife is lost in all of the confusion as a messenger.

There can be loneliness in a crowd of people if we do not have someone with whom we can share intimately. Marriage is made for that kind of belonging. Lonely people look outside the marriage relationship for a friend who cares to hear about them. I am not suggesting that a husband and wife should expect to meet every need for friendship, but I do feel that they should seek to cultivate their most in-depth friendship with one another.

Some suggestions of causes of loneliness (not unique to a minister's wife) that could be helpful to think about as a wife are:

- Lack of sharing intimately with your husband.
- Letting your husband define your role as a wife. It is a male guide for a female person. This would be an indefinite definition that subjects a wife to the whims of her husband. Also, it is based on emotion with very little thought about the female needs in the marriage. It may also shift the responsibility for the husband's happiness to his wife.
- Indefinite assignments or assignments of tasks with no plan to meet them.
- Expecting your husband to meet all of your needs — all of the time — not being responsible for yourself.
- Refusing to consider unconditional love (giving) or accepting your husband as he is and continuing to state who you are (wife).
- Not feeling you are being understood. Continue to give positive input about yourself.

Aimlessness comes about because neither husband nor wife knows for sure what the other is doing or the goals involved.

Separation does not always mean that a husband and a wife are residing in two houses or even in two bedrooms. Marriage reaches this stage when one says to the other, "You go your way and I will go mine because we can't seem to agree."

At this stage of decay, communication is often resorted to as a last hope. We can tolerate the pain no longer. We're forced to rebuild communication systems. Then we work back to the beginning. The beginning is to the last unresolved problem or conflict instead of the present problem. This is why many times when the body language is screaming out, "I have a problem" and he asks, "What is wrong?" she replies, "Nothing." That is true. It is not one wrong that is making her miserable; it is all of the unresolved conflicts stored up in her.

Where does communication begin? Most women tell me that it should begin with the husband. I think it should begin with the person who stopped it, but that is not always the case. Realistically, it begins with the one who wishes to communicate.

We all have a problem listening to something we do not want to hear, especially if we have heard it before. For instance, when a husband states a need that she does not want to consider, it is easier to say that he will not share with her than it is to accept what he is saying. I would challenge you to begin today to write down as many needs as you can hear from your husband in the next week. Most husbands keep telling their wives where they are, what they need, and how they feel. If a wife hears his comments and feels that she must do something to help or to correct him, she is not listening correctly. He is not telling her in order to get corrections but to let her know where he is. When he complains, "I am very tired," he is not asking his wife to arrange time off for him or a lecture on how he should take more time off. He is reporting a physical condition brought about by the day's activities. Sometimes he will ask her opinion for a female point of view.

Seek to be as current with your facts about your husband as you are the world news. Keep him abreast with how you are thinking. When you are sharing, remember how much easier it is to gather positive facts than it is to sort negative data. Usually one negative at a time is enough for anyone to be working on. Don't ask for input unless you are willing to consider the information given.

As you discover yourself and grow, share your findings from your perspective. Arguments are not necessary if the information received is considered a point of view or opinion of that person and not binding on you. Everyone has a right to his own viewpoint. Communication is not telling another person how he should be thinking or acting but is telling him about you. The listening part is not for correction but for firsthand information.

Sometimes we try to communicate by beginning our conversation with a question when we are not the least interested in an answer at this point. Does this sound familiar? A wife says, "Honey, what do you think *we* should do about the lawn?" Honey answers, "We are going to have it . . ." and the decision has been made in his mind. You are only getting ready to discuss the matter. You respond with your idea, and he immediately becomes irritated and accuses you of arguing with him. You are not arguing. You are giving your information after the decision has already been made in his mind. You asked for a decision. He gave a decision. Frustration! A better approach is: When you have some information to give, give it. If you are wanting to discuss it, say so. Do not come up with a question unless you want an answer.

Learning the skills of communication takes time, effort, and honesty with each other. Do not assume that you know your husband today because you have been married for a number of years. At a marriage retreat which my husband and I were directing, a couple had a humorous argument because he was eating green beans. She said, "You don't like green beans." He replied, "Yes, I do." The conversation went back and forth a few times with "No, you don't" and "Yes, I do." Then she turned to me and said, "His mother told me he would not eat green beans." This seemed a bit strange to me since they had been married twelve years. Her information was a bit out of date; plus, she had gathered it from the wrong person. To really be an honest opinion, it must come from the individual himself.

It takes real effort to communicate the kind of love that we choose to give to another. The constant need for affirmation ("Do you love me?") may be caused by a basic insecurity. Newlyweds are desirous of hearing how important they are to each other. They are eager to establish their value to the other. We need to grow trust and confidence in each other until we can hear and see without constantly checking to see if our performance has been acceptable.

A wife in the truest sense is to be giving *herself* and a husband is to be giving *himself* to the relationship. This gift should be accepted as presented. When this is done there is a desire to please the other and grow together.

There is no problem that cannot be resolved by a minister and his wife if they take seriously their commitment in marriage to one another. That is not to say they can always work through the intricacies of their personalities alone. Every marriage could be strengthened by outside assistance in conferences, retreats, groups, and private counseling. Breaking a marriage rarely corrects the problem. If we are interested in a better life, then we begin to work on our present needs. If you go—you will be there too and still have a problem to work through. Albert McClellan puts it this way: "Everywhere you go—there you are."

Several years ago an evangelist who was leading revival services in our church visited in our home. He asked me, "Do you like being a pastor's wife?" I questioned him with, "What do you mean? I like being Harold's wife—he is a pastor right now, but I would like being his wife whatever he does." The evangelist said, "No, that is not what I meant, but I know what you are saying. I was asking if you like the position of pastor's wife." I replied, "Only if I can define it."

A minister's wife's position is *wife* to her husband.

5
Little Reflections of Myself

" 'M' is for the many things she taught me" is typical of the reflections of what a mother means, how she is loved, and what she should be. These images of motherhood have been written about as much if not more than almost any subject. The label of motherhood is treasured by many and despised by some. One's own definition of the label mother is vital to her mental health.

Advice is given freely by total strangers when there is any call for correction between a child and her mother. But for the mother, care needs to be observed that this definition does not become idealistic but that it is realistic — one she can live by. Somehow we have become a people who set all of our goals out of reason and then comfort ourselves occasionally when we are worn down with "No one is perfect." Also, we go on trying to be perfect by impossible standards. Many times the mother of a minister's children has unrealistic expectations placed upon her from the congregation which add to her frustration.

There are many areas where a mother is not responsible. She is not responsible for doing her child's thinking and living. After a child accepts Christ, she is not responsible for aiding the convicting work of the Holy Spirit. She is not to use her children as a proof of her success. Children should not be set up as exhibit "A" to prove she has brought them up in the way the church members, her parents, her in-laws, the community, and the world in general think proper. She is not responsible to see that the father is what he is supposed to be to the child: nor is she to try to substitute for the father's absence.

A child is born with a mother and a father. Both are important from different perspectives. If only one parent had been needed, God would have designed it to be that way. The number of one-parent homes is rising yearly, but the complaint of one-parent responsibility has been something that goes on with both parents there. Many mothers do not feel fathers take care of fatherly responsibilities and try to make up for his deficiency. This only teaches the child false expectations about the father.

The father has a valid point of view. The mother has a valid point of view. These two resources need to be combined in order to meet the needs of the child in training and development. As a female she is only responsible for the mother label. Getting information together regarding anything from when to buy roller skates to which college to attend must be done in the best interest for the child from a mother point of view.

Most of our ideas of motherhood are built on sentimental traditions rather than Scripture. Many times children are taught by implication to worship, not honor, their mothers.

The guidelines for writing your definition of mother can be defined by Scripture by looking at the overall teaching of the Bible.

A mother is one who has given birth to a child. From birth on, she must learn how to be a mother to this individual child. She must make room in her life for the child. She must understand that she will be one of the child's greatest influences. She is responsible to the child, to God, and to herself to do her best to train the child as the mother.

Children take room. Young couples today are thinking more seriously about the responsibility of children. They plan physical room for the child and provide adequately the things that are needed. Time for the child in their lives is important, also. A child deserves to be planned for and wanted by parents. Children should not be treated as toys. They should not be used to add interest to the marriage.

The time requirements in child care need to be taken into consideration. The child not only needs time to be taken care of physically and mentally, but also emotionally and spiritually. Parents need to provide eighteen years for a child's development. A survey conducted by Ann Landers revealed that 70 percent of America's couples who responded would not have had children if they had it to do over again. If this is true, it further emphasizes that children require more of us than we realize. Maybe we have placed value on other things more than the time we spend with our children. Some preacher's kids have a way of getting attention with the parent when they feel everyone else comes first. Guests should not be allowed to rob children of their time with their parents.

Mothers become overwhelmed by the amount of time that is spent caring *for* children. They count this as time spent *with* the child. Personal time, on a one-to-one basis, is needed to let the child know his importance to the parent. This unhurried time, even though it may be done in five-minute blocks, is how some parents learn to enjoy their children as they grow. A child needs undivided attention from the parent to feel loved. One evening a week (15 or 20 minutes) per child can supply a wealth of information to the mother toward understanding the child's growth. It also provides a sense of worth to the child.

To try to be indispensable in a child's life is seemingly some parents' goal. Parents are to teach the individual child the knowledge and values he needs to know at each age. This approach brings enjoyment in each stage. A child requires freedom in order to grow. We would not bind our child physically or stunt the growth processes, but we fail to see that many times children are bound emotionally and not given room to develop. This lack of restraint of person needs to be exercised in the home first. This can be done by giving the child guidelines to work within and freedom to learn to be responsible for the decisions made. The child's primary influence and pattern for life is established in the home. That is not to say that the home is the only source of information.

One of the areas most minister's wives worry about is the criticism that comes from the fact that their children are minister's children. Children are capable of weathering criticism from others if they do not have a steady diet of it in the home. One child psychologist has stated that it takes one hundred compliments to repair the damage of one criticism of a child by a parent. When a child sees himself as valuable to his parents, he is well fortified for what comes his way.

Television is robbing the home of many of the patterns that parents should be teaching. Parents need to decide on the amount of time children will be allowed to watch TV programs and what programs will be viewed. This selection should be as carefully made as the food children eat. They are in the process of mentally and emotionally selecting models of behavior.

Attitudes are catching. The small child tends to accept the parents' attitudes as normal and right. In later years these parent patterns are adopted by the children as a life-style—sometimes modified but seldom rejected. However, some children come to despise the stance of their parents and reject the values they feel did not help them. A child who feels neglected because of the demands of the church on his parents' life will often refuse to become involved in the church.

Sunday can be the worst day of the week in some households. If attitudes, actions, and behavior are not consistent with Christian values, the child notices. Rushing because a mother has not planned ahead is a bad start to the day. With small children Saturday needs to be a time for choosing clothes and shoes to wear. Children can participate in this and look forward to Sunday morning. The organization not only makes Sunday more pleasant, but it also teaches the value of preparation for the Lord's day. The minister's home has added stress because of the active schedule of the day. Careful planning for a relaxed atmosphere is a good influence for the child.

Without preparation, Mother becomes a screaming mimee as she drags the kids to Sunday School and the worship services. She comes to worship and asks God's forgiveness. She also asks God to help her not to yell at her children and to be a good mother. Before Sunday dinner is over, screaming mimee is back! What is wrong? Doesn't God listen to frustrated mothers? Doesn't he want to help them?

She asked God to make her a good mother by some vague definition. What is causing her anger and frustration? Is she trying to fit the whole world into her schedule? It won't fit. Is her schedule and the things she wants to accomplish more important than the people in her home? Does she want her own way? Is she scheduling more than she can possibly accomplish? Maybe she needs to realize that the thing most apt to drive a parent wild is a child behaving like a child.

There must be autonomy of the person so that each child is allowed her own feelings if she is to mature into adulthood emotionally. A child's statement "I hate you and I am going to run away" may cause an angry response from many parents. Others just deny that the child really hates and feels desperate. What the child is trying to get across to the parents is anger, frustration, and loneliness. It is generally a shock method to get attention from the parents to help with problems and to get them to care. Children need assurance that they are loved.

How do you show love to a child? Too many parents try to say "I love you" with clothes, privileges, allowances, and other things. Time spent with a child, not on him, is what he needs. He needs respect as a person from parents: verbal approval every day, even if he has spilled his milk four times. He needs to be touched and held. He needs to be valued just as he is.

A child does not need to be lectured on having the right feelings. Parents must learn to accept a child enough to let him feel what he feels and slowly teach him self-control as he learns to deal with his feelings.

Sometimes children in a minister's home need permission to be ill. Because of so many schedules and meetings a minister's wife is expected to attend, a child may be pushed aside. Often church members' needs are considered above the child's needs, even in time of illness. A mother with three small children can count on three times as much illness as the mother with one child. Yet the mother of three may try to keep up the same amount of outside activities. The time that is given to a child when he is ill may be more important in the effectiveness of the mother than teaching a Sunday School class or putting in an appearance at a meeting. The health and welfare of the child is a responsibility given by God to the parents.

The responsibility to the child and to God is spelled out in Proverbs 22:6. Parents are admonished to "train up the child in the way he should go." This training, guiding, and directing takes time. It also requires mental and physical energy. The need is to see what direction each child should go. Also, there is a need to become emotionally involved with the child as he grows. It is a long-term assignment that is constant. Probably the most difficult part is deciding what to teach, how to teach, and when to move on to broader assignments.

Every child needs love. A child is influenced so much by the parents that he actually forms his concepts of God by how the parents relate to him. To love a child means to provide all of the child's needs. Since we can measure the physical needs, many parents use this as a standard for loving. As long as they provide a house, clothes, food, medical attention, education, and many extras, they feel they are showing love. The child needs personal attention from each parent, a program of discipline that is carried out consistently, verbal expressions of love, and personal time to grow spiritually and to picture God as a loving father, interested in her.

It is very difficult for ministers' kids to have a right picture of God because of all of the outside interference in their lives. Being treated as someone different, not like other children, plus the open criticism that is passed on to children as if they were to act as adults, and special adults at that, must be dealt with.

In many interviews that I have had with ministers' children, regardless of where they were age-wise, they agreed that they were expected to be model children as well as model Christians. They are reminded often by someone saying, "You had better act right; this is the minister's child," as if the child would report wrongdoings to God. Some try to control preacher's kids with, "You shouldn't do that. You should be the example to the other youth." Because of this pressure there needs to be extra love demonstrated to counteract these outside attitudes. Children need to be able to discuss with their parents these remarks made to them without the parents feeling they must correct them immediately.

Persons who see all children as little people who need tender loving care contribute much to encourage their maturity. When a child does not feel loved, he will evidence a constant demand for attention. Some are model children and use the attention as proof that they are loved. Others will be naughty or be overly active to call attention to their presence. The personal attention of a mother on a regular basis will assure the child of his place with her before the need arises to demand the proof.

Every child needs to know that he is valued as a person. The teaching of value of person is begun in the parent-child relationship. To try to fit an individual child in a mold is to destroy his worth in his own eyes. The minister's child has a secret battle going on as to his worth, due to the constant demands of the ministry. One young adult expressed it this way: "There was no privacy in our home. The job was always there. The phone was a frequent interrupter of dinner, conversation, quiet time, or whatever. Many times I questioned how important I really was to my parents due to their busy lives." On the other hand, there are many areas where the child is valued because he belongs to the minister. He meets people from near and far and is accepted by adults as a special person as they visit in the home.

Parents have the responsibility of helping a child develop healthy self-esteem. This is established as parents value the person of each child. Parents are representatives of God to a child. They must teach what is right and what is wrong. When there is respect and love shown for each individual child by the parents, healthy self-esteem is grown. Also, a foundation is laid for the child to be able to accept God's love for him as a person.

To base a child's worth on his performance is not to value him as a person. This causes much of the desire later in his life to perform his way into a right relationship with God. His thinking is, "Parents required it. God must require it."

Every child needs to grow to have confidence in himself. In each child there is ability and potential that must be recognized and plans made to develop them. Confidence in oneself shows emotional maturity. It is a recognition of one's own abilities not a comparison with others. As parents help a child begin to develop and learn new skills, they are moving that child on to independence and self-confidence. A mother can build in success experiences for children to help them develop in this area. One child should never be compared with another. When a child feels inadequate, he seeks to control others.

The new baby comes into this world wanting what he wants without regard for others. He is only interested in his own world. His world is made up of the space of his crib. He calls for everyone to turn their attention to him.

How common it is for a new baby to be in control of two adults and other family members. The entire schedule of activities begins to be centered around the baby. Parents are meant to be in control of the child in the child's early years and relinquish that control gradually as the child is trained to become responsible.

Bruce Narramore in his book *Help! I'm a Parent* makes a most helpful contribution to understanding that the power-struggle must not be entered into by the parent. Because of desire the child wants what he wants when he wants it. When parents take up the challenge, the child has control and feels insecure. According to Dr. Narramore the parents have accepted the challenge when their attitude becomes one of "I'll show you who is boss." This is evidenced also by the tone of voice used in talking with the child and the stubbornness exhibited by the child. The mother who gives instructions to "Go wash your hands" and continues to give the message over and over until she yells "Go wash your hands this minute" has lost control. The first direction should have been followed through by seeing that the child washed her hands. The mother should be teaching the child self-discipline.

A real mother-martyr is one who says or acts as if she is the sole influence in her children's lives. She equates her responsibilities as a teacher-in-residence as a burden, not a privilege.

Small children babbling, squawking, and competing all day are a drain on a mother's emotions. True, most men would not try to handle that assignment; but neither can most women without a great deal of complaining.

Who is in charge in your household? Dutiful Christian mother-martyr says, "My husband is head of this household" with her words. Her tone and actions tell you much more convincingly that there is really no leader present in this house, and the full workload is falling on her.

The truth of the matter is that the children are more often in charge than either parent. Check—who has the entire home in upheaval trying to meet their schedules? Who is complaining that they never get their own way—that no one loves them? "I never get to do—or go—or be like other people" immediately gives a parent the guilties. If the child is getting his way or making the parent feel apologetic or guilty, then the child is in charge. Guidelines given to children make them secure. Children need discipline in order to feel loved.

Avoiding the power-struggle is accomplished by working together as parents to establish what is to be taught to the child. When you know where you are going, you can have more confidence as a parent and state your answer to the question without feeling threatened.

It takes time to move a child to an independent state of being. A young foreign missionary, the mother of three children, ages eleven, nine, and five, shared her plan of work with me. She said she works alongside her children in the projects she assigns them. She gives them responsibility a little at a time. She works with them until she sees they have learned how to do the job. As they gain confidence, she works herself out of the picture and lets them work on their own.

Assignments should be used to build confidence and self-control. Many times assignments are not on the level of the child's comprehension; or they are given not to train but to relieve the parent of a job or to ease their conscience. Mothers sometimes give job assignments because others pressure her to be a good mother by their definition.

To point out what is done right is a strong motivating force. Try commenting on the right answers instead of the wrong answers. Avoid comment to others on your child's failures. Criticism is a destructive force that many try to use to motivate, only to find that it fails. The child may be hounded into a right performance but will not necessarily see his worth because of it. Criticism removes part of a child's material for accomplishment. To say "Why can't you settle down and learn?" suggests he is dumb. To ask "What problems did you understand on your test today?" would begin to teach from where he comprehends.

To arrive at a definition of a good mother we must, of necessity, think about discipline and punishment. There is confusion as the two words are used interchangeably. Even in some translations of the Scripture they are used as synonyms. Discipline means "instruction or training designed to correct misbehavior and develop the disciplined one." It is done in love to train and correct behavior. Hebrews 12 says it is a special love relationship used only with believers. God chastens (instructs), scourges (spanks), and rebukes (convinces—shows where we are wrong) his children. The punishment for our sins was borne by Christ. Correction is a sign of belonging to him and his love for us.

Punishment in the biblical sense refers to those who reject his Son. The three words used for punishment are full justice, imprisonment, and vengeance. These forms of punishment are set aside for those who reject the payment Christ made for their sins.

Using God's example, we understand that a person does not feel he belongs if he does not have discipline from those who are in charge of him.

Discipline takes time, creativeness, alertness, and patience. Parents must decide in the beginning what needs to be taught. The method of discipline should be considered in light of the particular time, child, and offense. Remember, discipline is carried out in order to teach the child. When the child is given the assignment of mowing the lawn, specific instructions are needed. To the child, "mow the lawn" could mean when you feel like it or sometime this week or running through the center of the lawn with the mower. Teaching the child to follow directions would mean giving a designated time and exactly *all* that is expected in cutting the grass. If the child chooses to take off with his friends at the stipulated time instead of mowing the lawn, there must be a plan to continue to teach following directions. The discipline should be in connection with the lawn if possible. It could be not allowing him to play with his friends until the lawn is completed.

In contrast to discipline, punishment is to get even or make the child pay for his error. It is generally done in anger. It is a looking back and not a building toward what is right. The fine line between the two is many times the attitude of the parent.

"You have forgotten the exhortation which is addressed to you as sons, 'My son, do not regard lightly the discipline of the Lord, Nor faint when you are reproved by Him; For those whom the Lord loves He disciplines, and He scourges every son whom He receives' " (Heb. 12:5-6, NASB).

There is instruction that regulates character; there is spanking and reproof that convinces of a better behavior in this Scripture passage. We need to be reminded that the child is being instructed about God, attitudes in life, values, and relationships as they observe parents. Sometimes seeing your child act as you do causes you frustration and anger. We as parents need to be sure our own behavior is consistent with what we are trying to teach.

Another kind of instruction that continues is communication. The child must be listened to for the parent to understand the child's point of view. We often assume a knowledge of what is right for the child without hearing his feedback. We try to guide him without really knowing where he is.

There's a high price tag on good communication. It means providing time for the child to learn to express himself. His worth is also established when the parents have enough time for the child to be heard. There needs to be listening without judgment, just listening for information. When a child feels he is being listened to, he feels accepted; and he is also willing to listen when you have something to share with him.

Parents have part of the information they need when they have listened to hear how the child sees himself. In order to feel loved, there is a need for the child to have limits or boundaries that are set by the parents. These guidelines cannot be established without both parents agreeing. A child senses, even if he has not heard, the disagreement between the parents.

Spanking is a form of discipline that needs to be administered with an inanimate object and not the hand. One reason for the use of the paddle is that it gives time for thought while you look for it. It should be used to help the child to remember the boundaries. It utterly fails to be effective when it is the only time the child is given attention, when the parents are not consistent, or when it becomes a power struggle. A spanking should never be given in anger.

There are other methods of discipline that can be effective. When a child is left to face the consequences of his actions, he learns quickly. We are so overprotective of our children that we disrupt the learning experience many times. We tend to protect them from any hurt and hope they will learn some other way. The best cure for a finicky eater is not coercion but an empty stomach. Regular meals and limited snacks help children to look forward to meals that are planned by mothers, not dictated by children's limited appetites.

The teenage driver can be convinced when he breaks the well-understood rules by forfeiting his keys for a period of time commensurate with the offense.

It is important to communicate the rules well. This does not mean stating them over and over. That is nagging to any age. We can help a child learn to listen. This is done when we take time by stopping all actions and sending a clear message and letting the child learn to be responsible for what he has heard. Mother must mean what she says enough to follow through with the discipline. If she does not follow through, she will not be believed the next time she instructs. The convincing comes when she keeps her word and the child feels the consequences.

Ministers' kids need to be allowed individual freedom like other children. God gives each person his own individual identity. As parents we must not deny what God intends for our children. Children do not need a continuous lecture on what they should or should not be doing. They deserve to have their intelligence recognized. They need to learn at an early age that they are responsible for the choices they make.

One area that wastes a lot of the mother's energy is the off-to-school scene. If a child is given an alarm clock and instructions on when to begin school, he will become responsible for arriving on time. Many times parents neglect the training of a child in early years and try to do a crash course in the teen years. It only makes everyone miserable and does not work. This is not to say that the project of training should be given up if there seems to be no success thus far. There is still time to communicate with an older child and let him know what he is going to be responsible for.

When parents agree on what they are seeking to teach, how long they plan to give for the lesson to be learned, and what method they plan to use, they are ready to begin. Remember, we can only work from where we are. That means where the child is, and that means as agreed as the parents can be. How well the program is understood and agreed on by all parties concerned determines to a great extent how successful it will be.

What is the mother of a sixteen-year-old responsible for? Her instructing, spanking, convincing time should be coming to an end, when many times it is accelerating. Turning loose of a young adult is almost impossible if it is seen as one act. If it is done a day at a time, it feels good. When a child has learned to dress she does not need to be watched over in that area but only helped when she thinks she needs it.

Most mothers experience several fears as the child moves closer to the time of leaving home. Have I taught him adequately? Did he learn sufficiently to be on his own? Will he be able to make good decisions by himself? Since his life has been sheltered, as the young adult goes out the door, there are multitudinous instructions. "Go to church. Make good friends. Study or work hard . . ."

The confidence parents have in their child begins to be very evident in the moving-out years. It is necessary for each child to begin to develop his own value system while he remains in the home in order to be prepared to build his own life. Parents dread the teen years because they see the child's expression of ideas as different from their own and call this rebellion. It is impossible to let children grow into these years without some ideas of their own. The rebellion is made necessary many times because parents feel the child should have exactly the same ideas and values they have. This time should be a moving back gradually of the boundaries until the child can stand independently.

When parents stifle a child by refusing to let any ideas be expressed other than the ones they agree with, they limit the discipline of communication. The child's struggle to mature emotionally is much more difficult. It is almost impossible for a young adult to emotionally mature with parents trying to control their thinking, feelings, and actions. Going to church is a big matter in the life of a preacher's kid. To some, the success of a minister's home is gauged by what the young adult chooses to do in relationship to the church when he leaves the home. This criterion does not afford self-determination to the young adult.

Some adults are emotionally handicapped because they have not been given the freedom to grow into becoming their own persons. If they choose to live their own lives, they feel they are dishonoring their parents and are guilt-ridden. If they perform as the parents wish, they are resentful of not being valued as an adult-person. They are trying to furnish purpose and happiness for the parents at the cost of neglect of their own life.

A mother who insists on majoring on her relationship as mother to her adult-children has the wrong major. She not only inhibits her children, but she is neglecting the relationship that made her a mother. A good mother must of necessity be a good wife first. An excellent way to avoid the pitfall of overmothering is to keep the emphasis on the marriage and to remember they are *our* children, not *my* children. "Till death do us part" is in the marriage vows, not the parent/child commitment. The time spent on a marriage will be time spent toward becoming better parents. Convention or conference time is a good place to exercise a turning loose of children when husband and wife go without the children. It furnishes a special intermission from family responsibilities. There is an occasion for uninterrupted emphasis on the marriage relationship.

The "perfect mother" is what we all strive to be. Children help us as they seem to remember extraordinary things. They give their mother the benefit of the doubt and see her as pretty great unless she is still trying to control their adult lives. A mother can cripple her rapport with her adult child by telling him, "Go get your hair cut. It is too long." Whether she realizes it or not, she is saying, "You are not acceptable to me with your hair that length."

There is a time to be training children in preparation for their life, and there is a time for letting children go. Some mothers go into a depressed state when the last child is gone, as if there is nothing left to live for. She has her value all wrapped up in being needed by her children. More and more mothers are getting the courage to talk about how great it is to have their children all independently functioning. As a mother gives out the freedom to be adult-child, she has some free time of her own. There is a time of adjustment after children have gone. This is a rearranging time. There needs to be some rescheduling, making new goals, and hopefully the completing of some old goals.

Fathers have a tremendous financial load lifted when children are self-supporting. Mothers have a new freedom not enjoyed for a number of years. Sometimes husband and children feel insecure because they fear she may become too independent. This causes a problem as they try to do her adjusting for her.

When the children leave, be good to yourself. Communicate how you feel. Now there is time for those quiet dinners for two that have been rare. There is much less time required to do cleaning, laundry, chauffeuring, and outside projects children always seem to have. There's usually more money. Gradually restructuring life-styles from family at home to husband and wife can be a challenge. While you work on your marriage, the children have a pattern for future use or encouragement to work on theirs now. It is easy for young adults to lean on the parents instead of establishing their own home. While it is painful, it is necessary for parents to help them by refusing to take responsibility for them. The earlier accountability is learned, the less impairment there will be.

A mother is always a mother. Her definition of relationship needs to be changed periodically. She says the kind of mother she wants to be. She says how she can encourage her children to become all that God has planned for them to be.

The following chart can be of use as a guideline to help define your label of mother in a more concrete way. Label a separate sheet of paper for each child. Provide the following information about each child:

1. Name of child.
2. Age of child.
3. The present need of the child.
4. The child's capabilities at present age.
5. Your responsibility to the child as you see it.
6. Your goals for the child.
7. The discipline (training) you think he needs.
8. The method you think proper.
9. Share your information as the child's mother with the child's father.
10. Come to an agreement as parents regarding the course of action so you can work together in the training of this child.

As you gaze into the looking glass you see Mother, as you spell it for yourself.

M — means me.
O — means only me.
T — means time consuming.
H — means health is needed (physical, mental, emotional, spiritual)
E — means every day energy required.
R — means right into adulthood.

Keep your definition current, and you will find more enjoyment as a mother.

6
Free to Be Me

The majority of the members of a church do not have difficulty defining what it means to be a member of their church. However, the general definition of church member seems not to apply to a minister's wife. Generally, there are further requirements expected of her.

When my late husband and I toured Israel we were told at Capernaum that the ruins of the two houses near the synagogue were those of Simon Peter and Matthew. Living near the place of worship, their wives may have had some of the same problems that minister's wives have today living next door to the church.

It may seem strange to some that we need to discuss the commitment of a minister's wife. It is a common problem to become insensitive to sacred things with which we work closely. A minister's wife lives daily with the spiritual problems of others. She may be tempted to use the same Scriptures and the same answers with others over and over without any freshness because she neglects her own relationship with God. Service to others will not suffice for her need of communication with God for herself and about herself.

Since there are no specific instructions for ministers' wives in the Bible, she must of necessity understand that she is subject to God just like everyone else. The majority of church members seem to think that a minister's wife automatically receives some kind of special transformation into maturity. Overnight she is expected to know all the Scriptures and how to apply them when she marries a minister. Others may think all she does is study and pray.

I once heard a woman say, "I cannot understand a minister's wife ever having a problem. They have the Scripture. What more do they need?" A wise person asked, "Do you ever have a problem?" She replied, "You know I do." "Do you have the Scripture?" "Well yes, but that is different." When asked, "How is it different?" all she could come up with was, "Well, it's just different." In some people's minds maybe it is different, but we know there is no special delivery of information for ministers or their wives.

In reality a minister's wife is not different than any other Christian. She cannot have salvation or maturity by proxy. Salvation comes by her accepting Christ as her Savior. Jesus came to intercede in our behalf before God. Through Christ we have direct access to the Heavenly Father. When he said, "I am the way, the truth, and the life; no one comes to the Father, but through Me" (John 14:6, NASB), he meant just that. All of the good works a minister's wife can do will not merit her way to God. She must come like all others, accepting Christ's gift of forgiveness of her sins and inviting him into her own life as her Savior. Growth comes slowly but surely as she commits herself daily to the study of his Word and prayer.

Private study plans are important to the minister's wife. Treat yourself to study guides and helps of your own interest. Begin by reading daily, at a quiet time that you make for yourself. Keep a notebook on things you learn and applications you need to make. It is really a spiritual growth diary. One chapter a day as you read through a book of the Bible will build your relationship with Christ. Be careful not to make this a rigid discipline just to say you have done it. Do it for your own personal time in order to relate to the Lord.

Prayer is such a vital part of a believer's life that Paul said in 1 Thessalonians 5:17 that it should be a continuous relationship between God and you. Jesus said in Matthew 6:6 that it is a very private matter. To me, entering into the closet simply means that each person has the privilege of being herself before God and being completely understood by God.

Private prayer is an excellent time to learn who you are and what God wants for you as his child. It is the time to tell God how you see yourself, how you feel about everyone and everything around you. Complete honesty is possible because he knows you and loves you. This relationship keeps you from speaking hastily when you are angry.

This is a time when you can say how unfair it seems when another has mistreated you; then God has an opportunity to guide and help you. He will remind you of what he has said in his Word. Sometimes he reminds you that he loves the other person too. At other times he reminds you that he is in control and that justice is to be left in his hands. He has reminded me from time to time that he has not appointed me to a judgeship.

Even the bigger part of anger can be dealt with between you and God. If it has not been communicated to others, let God help you sort it all out. There will be no resentment stored.

Prayer is also a time to lay your plans out before God for his approval and his "well done." If we take the prayer Jesus taught his disciples as an example, the greater part of our praying will be for self. Prayer is personally relating to God.

With God's Word, his Spirit, prayer, and your involvement, victory is assured on a day-to-day basis for a lifetime—into eternity.

The two labels Christian and church member should fit together very well. For the minister's wife the church member label is sometimes painful because in a sense she is a member of the church by assignment rather than choice. Her husband is called to a field of service. If she is to stay married (and we hope she will), she goes along.

If her church membership and her effectiveness as a person are important to her, she will share her opinions and evaluations with her husband before the decision is made to move to a new place of ministry. Sometimes it is a temptation for the minister's wife not to become involved in the decision-making process. She waits until she arrives on the field and sees how she likes it and then gives her opinions. Then it's too late!

It is extremely difficult for some women to move. They close themselves off from their husband and family to avoid being negative. They may feel that they cannot be heard because of their negative feelings.

A few wives are fearful of speaking up because they might over-influence their husband in his decision. A wife who does not participate in the decision-making process is negligent in her contribution to the marriage. Why should he be asked to make a marriage decision alone? Others will try to persuade; why not the one most involved? A wife should realize that to influence her husband does not mean trying to get her own way. It means sharing ideas and feelings about the move from her point of view.

Denominations differ in the method of changing fields of service. There is room for input in the majority of them. To some ministers' wives the sight of a pulpit committee is threatening because it signals the possibility of moving. The annual board meeting is dreaded by others. The same committee or board would be welcomed by ministers who feel their assignment is finished. A husband and a wife need to agree before talking to a committee as to how interested they are in moving. Questions need to be open and honest. Many anxieties could be avoided by working through difficulties together so they can face the new situation as a unit. Wives, also, have a tendency to feel they must be the protector of the children during a change of address. This feeling may stem from a disagreement about the children in other areas.

There are far less problems in deciding whether to move if there is communication between husband and wife all of the time. Remember, he is the minister and usually will have strong impressions when his present task is completed. A wife recognizes this too when she has been listening to him. The wife needs to question freely and make her input before the final decision is made. It is her life, too. God is interested in each person involved.

A phrase that is heard too often is, "He decided not to move because of his wife." Most of the time this statement is made in a derogatory manner. What is more important than a husband and wife standing together? In all probability the husband has considered all the information and made a final decision. He would not be nearly as effective without consideration of the one he is bonded to being important to him.

In some people's minds there is a mysticism about being called to another field of service that disregards the need of a man to provide emotional security for his wife and family. Ministering to the needs of others at the expense of one's own family weakens his testimony. It is more difficult to live a consistent Christian life in the home than it ever is in the church. It is more difficult in the church than in the community. When we can show love (by God's definition) in marriage and family, Christ is believable to the people in the fringe areas of our lives. The more overall consideration given before a move of the good to be accomplished, the more effective it will be.

A move to a new church can be devastating to women who have a problem making new friends. It can be upsetting to children, although some children are excited by the adventure and opportunity of a new environment as well as new people in their lives.

Special care needs to be given to teenagers in the moving process. They need extra time and attention for a while, as well as much involvement as possible in the actual moving.

There is usually some difficulty for family members in moving from a small town or village to a metropolitan area. Identity is something of a family image in a smaller environment. In the city it is every person for himself. This is hard on children who have depended on the parents' position in the community to make a place for them.

When the reverse is true and a move is from the city to a small town, some children rebel at not having their own identity apart from their father's position. The problems of transition can be eased when parents provide explanations to children for the move and give consideration to their feelings. A mother shared this experience with me. The week following her husband's resignation, their ten-year-old daughter would come to their bed in the night crying, "I don't want to move." She took the time to tell her, "I know how you feel. I hate to leave my friends too." Her daughter was able to move with less difficulty because her mother listened sympathetically. It is so easy to get caught up in moving the things that we forget the people who are hurting and need attention.

A move is much more difficult for the wife who is artistic or has a profession. If she is an accomplished organist and moves to a church that already has an organist, the opportunity for her to use her talent is limited. Accepting a position to play for another congregation may be quite unpopular with her church. This causes a wife to seek expression of her musical ability outside the church. For some wives the answer is to give up music. Her needs and her talents are important to God and require a place of expression. They should be taken into consideration by both husband and wife as they share together in new opportunities of service.

The church is God's plan. It is coming under attack constantly. Some see attendance (called faithfulness) as their main function in church membership, disregarding personal commitment to God. We need to study to refresh our memories on what God says the purpose of the church is in Acts 2:42—Bible study, fellowship, worship, prayer. The church is to be a learning center, a place of sharing and encouragement, and a congregation in group worship. Because of the church's meaning to Christ, we need to guard these true concepts. We are to be faithful to him. Worship takes concentration, energy, preparation, and involvement. Any believer is empty without it.

Serving from an empty church-related, not God-related, life soon is evident. It results in no joy, no enthusiasm, no zeal, much criticism, a muddled gospel, and religious sounds but not deeds. Our lives are equipped for service by relating personally to God. A minister's wife needs to be aware of the warning signs of her service becoming drudgery and make space to update her relationship with God.

A good way to arrive at a definition of church member is to begin by listing the ways you can be faithful to God in his church where you are a member. The list might read: honest, good attitude, willing to be of service in a named area, aware of other's needs (name the needs that you have the resources to meet), equipped to minister as (name where), contribute time (say how much), talents (list), and finances (what amount).

A Southern Baptist survey in 1976 by the Research Services Department of the Sunday School Board indicated that two-thirds of the ministers' wives who responded felt that they were simply Christians with the same responsibilities as any other Christian. How does this attitude hold up in practice?

Being married to a minister is in some ways like being married to a man in his own business with a board of directors and every customer a stockholder. Not quite—but similar. Surely when you are married to someone you want to see him succeed. When your livelihood is involved, you have a greater concern. Is it possible to say that we are not any more involved than any other Christian? It sounds good to others, and it is a self-pep talk to yourself; but the involvements go much deeper. The success of your husband, the financial security, the family's daily welfare depend largely on the church. A faith of great depth is required not only in God, but in the people of the church. It is commitment without a contract with a general job description. You are trying to read minds which are constantly changing. You are being bombarded by an avalanche of methods and materials. Little time is left to decide who you are and where you are going. The church becomes a part of you, and you become a part of it.

Every wife of a minister could profit by being practical and listing her contributions that she wishes to make to the church. Unless she defines what she is willing to give, she cannot have the joy of giving. She will feel that it is required of her, and resentment is sure to follow sooner or later.

Of all the members of the church, she is the one most closely associated with her husband. In relationships she has the first place — wife. She may see herself as a team worker, a background person, the associate pastor, the pastor's pastor, or any other category she may choose. The important thing is that she must decide what her roles are.

Luke 6:38 is a good motto: "Give, and it will be given to you; good measure, pressed down, shaken together, running over, they will pour into your lap. For whatever measure you deal out to others, it will be dealt to you in return" (NASB). We are told to give God's love in proportion to the amount he has given to us. When we give his love away, he refills us until his love overflows. This brings real joy in service. When a cup flows over it must be full inside, and the overflow touches the outside of the cup into the saucer — out on the table and onto the floor. The minister's wife's relationship with God is where the supply emanates, and the overflow will touch her husband (the other side of the cup), other believers (the table), and on into the world (the floor). She could fill the entire area around her as long as she accepts God's love for herself.

Many times the wife is the only person her husband has to share with. There are things about himself that he should only share with his wife. Although we can all wish for ideal circumstances where there is an adequate staff with everyone working together toward the mission of the church, these circumstances rarely occur. What we would really like is an effortless blessing resulting from easy service.

Many churches are functioning with an inadequate staff. No business asks as much coverage from one person as does a church. The churches with large staffs many times are facing the same problem—being responsible for too broad an area. There is often a lack of real interest among ministers for one another. There are few who have the privilege of wise, confident counsel when it is needed. A minister is cast in a role by tradition that includes certain expectations. His wife must not add to the judging of his performance as another church member.

Her most important area of church service is to provide a close, honest, relationship with her husband. She should not assume a personal responsibility for all the church needs. She is to be a person who cares for, prays for, and relates to her husband; and on other occasions she ought to contribute a female point of view. Her best contribution in many situations is to be a good listener. She does not need to try to find solutions or make corrections unless she is asked to. A husband may ask for help to solve a particular problem. His wife may be tempted to use the occasion to tell him how to live his life.

One example was a minister having trouble expressing himself. He continued making grammatical errors in sermons on certain words over and over. His wife called it to his attention. He thanked her and said he appreciated her help. She took his appreciation to mean that she was to become his teacher and corrector. She began reporting his errors as soon as they reached the car after each service, causing a tension between them. It hindered her worship because she was more interested in sentence structure than she was content. His anger finally led to his saying, "Don't ever correct me again."

Because she cares, a minister's wife must share if she feels her husband needs help. Opinions and insights should be expressed in the right spirit and at an appropriate time. But state them *only once, please*. He then is responsible for the evaluation and application of the advice.

Some wives feel that they are expected to assist their husband in his ministry as an additional unpaid staff member. Two ministers for the price of one can injure a church as well as the husband and wife. It makes the husband feel he is inadequate for the task. More often a wife becomes directive instead of supportive. She feels everyone should do more since she is giving so much for free. When she asks others to take responsibilities and they decline, she takes it as rejection of her. The church will become educated to expect something for nothing. When this happens and the next minister's wife does not choose to work in Vacation Bible School, certain members of the church will feel she is not interested in the church.

I was questioned by a woman at a retreat, "How does your church feel about your writing?" I guess I looked puzzled. I asked, "What do you mean, how do they feel?" She said, "I mean your being away leading others in retreats?" My reply was, "Fine," which may or may not be true. Since I was an individual believer, not employed by the church, and I was carrying out my accepted responsibilities, I never really thought to ask the church for approval. My husband and I agreed on my schedule. I assumed his approval was sufficient. If someone in the church were to have questioned me, I would have been glad to share with them how I felt about what God was doing in my writing ministry.

The only motivation some ministers' wives seem to have for Christian service is to fill the need others can't or won't fill. Others try to please their husband or to protect their husband from criticism. A wife needs to find her place of service and fill it according to her definition of what she has to give and what she chooses to give to God. She should not serve in order to gratify others. Nor should she serve to show-off to make others feel guilty. She should not fear serving because of how others see her service. Many self-righteous people try to put down others who serve by always having them check their motives. Let your motive be to serve him. "Let each one do just as he has purposed in his heart; not grudgingly or under compulsion; for God loves a cheerful giver" (2 Corinthians 9:7, NASB).

In my search for the main need among pastors they have said to me, "I do not need my wife to be my pastor. I need much more. I need her to be my wife."

Another contribution a wife can make as a church member is to demonstrate her love by caring, beginning at home. She can care about her husband's schedules, his health, his needs, his security, his commitment, his recreation. However, she should not try to take charge of his life. Rather, she should care about every facet of his life.

When a husband begins to hurt, there are two avenues a wife can take. One is to move close to share that hurt with him. The other is to move away and to put distance between them so the hurt will not be so painful for her. The wife may become frustrated because she is not able to lift his burden or relieve his pain. She is not free to find a solution because it is his problem. There is added stress being in a position where there is little room for correcting what needs correcting, even though she may have the skills to meet the problem. However, she is privileged to share the real person he is and know how to pray for him intelligently. She can ask for God's wisdom to see the needs she can meet in his life—such as always listening to him. She may be able to provide a fresh viewpoint. This female opinion needs to be given skillfully as a gift and not as a command. If she feels she is being left outside because of his first love (the church), she must state clearly where she is emotionally.

She needs private time to communicate to her husband what she has to offer in talents in the church. As both minister and husband, he is probably aware of some skills that she does not even recognize. Let him challenge her to move into areas where he sees her capabilities. He does not need added burdens of trying to discover her resourcefulness laid on him. He cannot be as adequate for the task if she withholds information about herself from him.

Your time is assigned to you by God. You choose how you will use it, whether teaching, planning, serving, or being. Encouragement is something that you can give and that everyone, especially your husband, needs.

Be careful! Don't get confused by all of the outside voices. God is trying to develop you for his glory, not trying to make you like someone else. A missionary told me that it had been announced on her new field of service before she arrived that she would be playing the accordian, just as the former missionary had. She arrived and quickly explained that she had never even held an accordian in her hands.

If you can't, you can't! Don't feel guilty about it. You are there to give what you have. You cannot give what you do not have. I learned this lesson as a young inexperienced wife of a minister just completing college. The associational missionary appeared at my door on Saturday afternoon. He had a large bundle of papers in his hand. "You are to lead a one-hour conference for teachers of youth next Monday morning." I protested. I tried to explain that I had never even been to an associational meeting as an adult, and I had never taught youth. "I cannot possibly do it," I explained. He ignored my words and left the bundle of papers.

Under pressure I dug in. I decided I could use the program time showing those in attendance the materials the missionary had given me. I was a nervous wreck when I arrived at the meeting. I was pleased nobody showed up for my group. From the experience I learned two lessons quickly and painfully. When I say no, I do not go ahead and do it. When I ask someone to do something, I always explain the assignment and give them room to say no if they do not feel they are ready.

Dealing with people in the church is no small assignment. First John is written to Christians on how important it is to love those in the Christian community. I have been questioned as to why John did not emphasize loving the lost world. My answer is simple. If we can love those close to us in the church, with our many differences, we will have little problem loving a lost world. The New Testament is full of instruction to care for and encourage one another as believers. Some people are surprised that this compassion does not come naturally in the package with salvation. Ministers' wives feel guilty when they cannot sympathize the same with each member of the congregation. The remorse is relieved when they understand the love called for.

There are two special words translated *love* in the Bible. The first, *phileo*, means a warm, tender feeling—as in friendship. The other, *agapao*, means a God-kind of love. It is the kind that you decide to give to another by choosing to be patient, kind, approachable, noncritical, seeing people's better side, and nonjudgmental. One feels doomed when she thinks it is necessary to have a warm, tender feeling toward everyone. There is relief in *agapao* love because she can choose to be kind to a person and not feel obligated to be a close friend.

Lovely people are easier to love. To love these whole individuals is no great strain. In fact, it is enjoyable most of the time. We can have a warm, friendly feeling toward them. However, even with love, there are differences. The uniqueness of God's creation and the differences in backgrounds cause us to have varying points of view. We are challenged in the Scripture to let each person be united into the making of a whole body (Eph. 4:16). As the wife of a minister you do not have the assignment to pull all of these differing views together. Yours is to be supportive. Be a builder, not a destroyer. Love enough to see what is good, lovely, and praiseworthy in a person (Phil. 4:8).

Let's face it: there are people who bore you to tears and others who are difficult to love. There is no warm, tender feeling toward them. Do these make you feel guilty? Do you feel like you are not even a Christian sometimes because you cannot have the right feeling toward some of God's children? It was a great day in my life as a minister's wife when I realized I was using the wrong test of love for evidence of my relationship to God. He says for me to be patient with others and kind to them and quit basing my love on what I feel toward them.

Who are these unlovely ones? God's children. He loves them as much as he does me. A friend who is a new Christian attended a swapmeet where people of every description gathered. She looked at the masses and said, "How could you, God? Really? All of them?" Yes, his unconditional love is for everyone. His command to us is to let people have their individuality and uniqueness. It takes growing to allow people this freedom to be themselves, but God gives us the desire when we are committed to him. We need to put forth the effort.

Some persons say that what is needed is for a minister and his wife to treat everyone alike. That is impossible because everyone is different. Treating everyone alike would be similar to caring for a child who has the measles as you would one with a broken arm. They need different kinds of treatment in order to be well. You don't set the measles or use lotion to ease a broken bone. We are individuals. Every person has his own set of needs. We need to relax and minister to the needs of individuals with our God-given skills and resources.

Ministering to individuals has hazards. One peril is becoming so involved in helping a person that there is too much entanglement. Infidelity is a common temptation to those who minister because of the close association.

A young minister's wife came to me seeking consultation to find perspective after her husband had confessed an affair with a mutual friend. She said, "I saw my friend taking time with Joe, talking with him, appealing to him, spending time at our house—as my 'friend' too—that was what was so hard to sift out. I considered her a sister and enjoyed doing things with her. I felt I was helping her with problems, being a friend to her." Underneath, this minister's wife resented the close relationship and treated it as a jealousy on her part. She even thought of herself as unchristian because she was unwilling to share Joe's time with those who needed him. She said to me, "I did not know how to share adequately what I felt, but I knew I felt left out." These feelings are common when infidelity is suspected.

In a large group of ministers' wives the question was raised, "What about the other woman? We need to know if there is anything we can do." No wife is completely free of the possibility of women seeking confidant time with her husband because of the nature of his work. The agreement among the ministers' wives after much discussion was that the husbands need more information and discussion of the problem. Some felt there was very little they could do to stop the other woman or help their husband.

A wife needs to be encouraged to be open with her husband about what she sees and feels in another woman's conduct in relationship to him. The wife should not ignore the woman who is paying affectionate or intimate attention to her husband because she does not know how to tell her husband what she feels. Amy said to me, "I was afraid he would think I was questioning his integrity or fidelity. It was like attacking him to even hint that the woman had ulterior motives. I was afraid he would think I did not trust him, and I really do."

She does need to take precautions not to accuse her husband. She should simply report to him what she sees from a female point of view and how it makes her feel. She needs to help her husband have confidence in her judgment because she is interested in him. She can make him aware that women better understand how and what other women are communicating.

They both need to discuss and to accept the fact that there are women who: (1) have poor marriages where their sexual needs are not being met; (2) have spiritual problems for which they want answers; (3) are not as interested in what God's Word says as they are having their self-esteem restored; (4) are seductive and are trying to win the attention of the minister; (5) honestly want the male counsel of their minister.

The "other woman" in a minister's life more often than not has her sexual feelings mixed up with her spiritual feelings. Her feelings are centered in the person who helps her to *feel* better about God and about herself. Her worth is wrapped up in her desirability to others. These facts are danger signals to the minister and to his wife.

A wife who is being herself, communicating with her husband, and seeking to meet his needs does not spend her time comparing herself with others.

Infidelity is not a one-sided issue. There is the temptation of a wife becoming involved with another man. When a minister's wife is lonely or feels that she is not understood or appreciated, she is vulnerable. 1 Corinthians 10:12 says, "Therefore let him who thinks he stands take heed lest he fall." This Scripture applies to sexual weakness as well as other types of sin.

There are areas that need attention if "the other person" is going to be kept out of the marriage.

Communication is vital to building a good husband/wife relationship. The Dear Abby columns are full of requests seeking solutions to problems caused by inadequate communication. It is as if we do not know or cannot bear to share ourselves with those we love. This withholding of vital information is detrimental to both partners and causes the suffering of loneliness in marriage. Get to know each other. Keep your information current.

Are we asking the impossible in marriage? Is a husband or a wife to supply all of the other's needs? This would be making another responsible for physical, spiritual, emotional, and sometimes mental needs. This is a parasitic existence. Both must be contributors to the marriage. Since it is difficult to have close friendships with members of the congregation, ministers and their wives tend to have a greater dependency on each other.

I saw a cartoon in which the minister was asking the groom, "And do you promise to love, honor, cherish, obey, respect, uplift, understand, encourage, involve, revitalize, inspire, admire, entertain, relate to, communicate with . . . " The groom just stood there with his finger in his mouth, looking dumbfounded. We each need to bring our own contribution of love, trust, and confidence to the marriage. We also need to continue being the best of friends.

Criticism takes its toll on a relationship. To be a reformer of another is to say, "You are not satisfactory to me as you are." It is also saying, "I am a perfect judge of what God intended for you to be." Cultivating right attitudes toward yourself will help you give your husband room to be himself and makes him comfortable being with you.

Symbolic infidelity is present in marriage when oneness is not being cultivated. "Do you take this man to be your lawful wedded husband" is a legal agreement and a vow to God to build a good marriage. Any person, organization, job, hobby, or thing that takes first place means unfaithfulness to one's mate. Sometimes a minister's wife will become involved in her own direction because of the time her husband spends away from home. Refusing to make some changes in her life to build the marriage means she will be missing a chance for real growth and enjoyment. Rights are not the question. It is to build or not to build, to be faithful or unfaithful. There is no middle ground. It takes conscious effort and keeping your priorities straight to give first place to your mate. With the number of requests for a minister's wife's time, it is difficult to change plans and go with your husband when he expresses a desire for you to be with him.

Not being concerned about your husband's needs leaves room for involvement with others. Sometimes you get so overconcerned about your own needs that you cannot hear your husband sharing his needs or decide what you can do to help him. Because of the battle between the sexes that goes on subtly, many women are unwilling to try to meet their husband's needs. A wife is often afraid the husband will take advantage of her. She may fear she will give more than she will receive. When genuine love and consideration are given to another, there is no need for a measure to see who is doing the most.

These problem areas are things that cannot be ignored as potential pitfalls in your marriage. Unfaithfulness comes about in every marriage from time to time when we put something or someone ahead of our mate.

Lack of communication, overdependency, criticism, symbolic infidelity, or not being concerned about your husband's needs are all areas of danger. But the primary danger is one of growing apart and not building together.

Will the real minister's wife please stand up? There is some role-playing being done by every minister's wife, with the exception of those who have totally rebelled. Some believe that honesty means to get everyone told off and straighten everyone out. However, you can be real with people only if you have yourself in control enough to know who you are and what you want for your life. There is only substitute living, not real living, if you are trying to live the life of another. For exuberant living, learn to be comfortable being yourself.

A minister's wife who is a positive person has plenty to give, but saying one thing and feeling another will get her into emotional trouble. There can be many resentment builders she must deal with. The little nagging one will drain her energy. Here are some to avoid:

(1) Being a message deliverer, thinking she is responsible for seeing that her husband does what is asked of him.

(2) Filling in where he is lacking, rounding out his place of service instead of having her own place.

(3) Always explaining her husband's or her own point of view as if it needed defending.

(4) Being apologetic for her use of time or money.

(5) Trying to fit into a mold others have made and always seeming not to measure up.

(6) Listening to people who do not have or have not had her particular problem, saying, "There is an easy answer or you have a bad attitude."

(7) Expecting her to do (perform) before there has been time to be (character).

(8) Not making time for herself even though she says everyone deserves some private time.

To be a real person as well as a church member, she must stay in touch with her feelings and share them with her husband so he knows where she is at all times. Feelings are a part of her life, and she needs to face them in order to know what to do with them. However, any time she begins to live her life on a feeling basis alone, she is in trouble. There must be acceptance of her feelings, but there must also be proper control and use of her feelings. When a minister's wife feels someone is unfair to her children, she should feel free to express her dissatisfaction without telling the other person what they must do.

There is probably no area that is more difficult to deal with than criticism toward those we love. This area is a very sensitive one for the minister's wife due to the number of people she and her husband must relate to. Much criticism of his ministry is given in the form of suggestions of how it should have been done after a project is under way. Sometimes criticism comes in the form of messages or questions that need to be asked of her husband. Instead of delivering a coded message to your husband, politely ask the person to speak directly with him. You want him to get the correct message.

Also, refuse to deliver ill will for another. People will not be nearly so anxious to complain or to criticize a minister directly as they are to deliver the message through his wife. If a person insists on registering a complaint, say, "I do not have anything to do with that. I cannot help you. You will need to talk with" and give the name of the person to see. Be sure that you give your opinions or suggestions to your husband in private. Many times the congregation tends to deliver messages in the same way they see the minister and his wife communicating. If she sends a humorous message to correct her husband about the content of his sermon, the congregation will feel it is permissible for them.

One injury that many seemingly well-meaning church members inflict on the minister's family is the insulting things that are said to ministers' children. Sometimes I think they do not realize that children understand even more than the words implied. Children get a full picture. They intuitively know who likes and who dislikes them or their parents.

A minister who is a minister's child gave an emotional testimony in church several years ago. He rejected Christ until he was twenty years of age. He left home because of things that he had seen and heard in the church as he grew up. Even a joking kind of criticism of a minister's family can often be the most cutting kind because others are laughing at the hurt.

In preparation for this book I interviewed several minister's kids. The effect of such criticism was very evident in their young lives. They carry scars. Most recover. Others withdraw. Jody, one young woman, became very emotional as she shared how different church members would tell her mother how she should behave. As a result, her mother made a constant effort to help her daughter be perfect.

Jody said tearfully, "I have always been an adult. There was never any room to be a child. I still find myself trying to please everyone, and I just can't do it anymore." As a mother I can say, "Do not add your own criticism to everyone else's." Children need reinforcement from you. Never make them feel they must be examples for others. Help them grow to have confidence in themselves. Hear what they share with you because they must have a place to sort out genuine feelings.

The Pharisees misused God's Word to set standards of behavior for everyone and to declare themselves as judges.

As you mature, live by God's standard for you. Everyone is not where you are. Some are more mature; some are less so. Your main concern should be to press on from where you are, not where others think you are supposed to be.

A minister's wife is working from an impossible place if she operates her life as others see her. God knows where she is, and he wants to guide her from here. The most important thing is that the fruit of the Spirit be evident in her everyday life—love, joy, peace, patience, kindness, goodness, faithfulness, gentleness, self-control.

On hearing a direct or an indirect criticism, usually we pick it up and tend to believe that everyone in the church feels that way about us.

If we are not careful we will develop *Hamanitis*. In the book of Esther, Haman was the man appointed by the king over all of the princes. He became obsessed with the fact that one man, Mordecai, did not agree with him. Haman was a man with position. Even though he had direct access to the king, he spent all of his time trying to figure out a way to get rid of Mordecai. His concern for one man's criticism resulted in his premature destruction.

Criticism is only destructive to you if you begin to set your life's goals by it. God gives every person the right to his own opinion. He only holds us responsible for our own opinion.

Indirect criticism is gossip. It should not only be avoided, but it should be rejected as invalid when delivered to us. If a person delivered a package marked *Bomb,* I would not just stand there holding it; nor would I begin to unwrap it to see if it really was a bomb. I would get rid of it where it would not cause harm to myself or anyone else who might be in that vicinity. Similarly, another person's remarks spoken by a second party are going to be added to simply because they have been interchanged. Each person's marks will be left on events. You cannot handle another person's feelings and thoughts without mixing your own feelings and thoughts with them.

There are two ways to dispose of criticism. The first is to do a quick inventory to see if you may have a blind spot in your thinking that needs to be remedied. This needs to be in line with where you are going in your life, not where someone else thinks you should be going. If it is a piece of information you can use—use it. If not, discard it. Do not dwell on it. The junking of criticism needs to be done as quietly as possible. Be careful not to contaminate those close to you. Protect your husband, children, and friends by not repeating hurtful remarks.

The second way is to forgive the one who is misinformed or who has such poor self-esteem that they must put others down to see any value in themselves. Matthew 18:21-35 is a passage of Scripture that needs to be read often. We are asked to forgive others as Christ has forgiven us. It helps to keep our perspective on forgiveness in relation to the Scripture, not what everyone else is doing.

A minister's wife has a special vantage point from which to serve as a member of the church.

Where you are today is your place of service. God has assigned you to your own territory. Ambassadors of our country are appointed by the president and approved by the Senate to serve as representatives of our country. The president does not appoint an ambassador, then go for him to make all of his decisions. He does his own representing.

He is sent because he represents the United States and wants the best for his country.

"We are ambassadors for Christ" (2 Cor. 5:20, NASB). We are citizens of his kingdom, children of God. He even goes with us to guide us and strengthen us. We have the assignment to represent him. We are forfeiting our ambassadorship or relinquishing our place when we refuse to stand for him in the place where we are.

As a minister's wife you are not a flower that is allowed to grow in a secluded place. You must bloom along the pathway where everyone looks at you and bumps against you. It is a privilege to be where you can be the light of the world and the salt of the earth. God has equipped each one with what we need to serve effectively where we are. A pulpit committee asked a prospective minister what positions his wife filled. He did his wife a favor when he replied, "She will come to you as my wife and a new church member who will need time to find her place of service." Develop *your* life. Do not try to explain yourself to others. God has promised you the strength to succeed.

7
A Wearer of Many Labels

Webster's Dictionary says a homemaker is a woman who manages a home. Yet the common expression for this role is housewife. As we look at this label there are two points to consider. Wife is not a term to be used in relation to a house. A wife is in relationship to a husband. She is wife wherever she is—in the house or out. Homemaker does not necessarily mean housekeeper but can include that area of work. The word in marriage is a plural word—homemakers. There is a husband part and a wife part to homemaking.

A keeper of the house as used in Titus 2:5 is one who is to manage the household under her husband's leadership. To understand the husband's leadership role, see chapter 5 in *Man: Responsible and Caring.* This management under the husband's leadership is for the purpose of harmony in the home; it will make a good marriage evident and God's Word believable.

Management of a household has many areas of responsibility—to control, guide, direct, conduct, administer, handle, and succeed in accomplishing. It is a wife's privilege to make plans for having the kind of household that she wishes.

The kind of house she has to work in limits her freedom to be creative. If the house where she will do her homemaking is provided by the church, one of her decisions is already made. Now she must decide what to do with this conglomerate of someone else's ideas to make it into a suitable base for her family.

The adequacy of the house, location, and condition are part of the frustration of moving. The furniture rarely fits. There are adjustments to be made. In a few instances the house is furnished; that poses a challenge for her decorating skills. Sometimes it takes a tremendous imagination to see any possibilities for personalizing a pastorium. It does not feel like home until you have lived there a while and the house begins to take on the personality of the family.

The idea of trying to fit the house to every family who will ever live there is impossible. The house is your home, and it should be considered so. The next family can work things out to their liking. The blahs of decorating for the unknown family is sterile living. A home shows others the care and interest in living of those who live in it. If the house is neutral in color, the homemaker needs to use the things that belong to her to add interest and accent. One benefit in decorating will be taking the items with her when she goes. You may not be able to change the location of your home, the school, or the church. The weather may not be to your liking. But you can rearrange furniture, take a picture down that has been hanging there a long time and replace it or rearrange it, or make or buy a new floral arrangement. Try growing flowers in your yard or in pots in your house.

There is the proverbial problem of trying to manage a home by way of the church committee. There is probably nothing more irritating. A good relationship with the chairman of the committee or one of the members of the committee who is a good fixer-upper helps. Keep your requests on a friendly basis, not with a "You should have taken care of this yesterday" attitude. It is diplomatic to make requests for home repairs when a cup of coffee, piece of pie, and warm fellowship follows. If the problem is a stopped-up drain, it expedites matters to call the committee chairman and ask which plumber should be called when the chairman's permission is needed.

More ministers are being given housing allowances and are buying their own homes. This too can have its frustration. There is rarely enough money to buy a suitable home; plus, there is the need to locate in a convenient place. These are good problems to have and should be welcomed since the church is giving the minister and his family the opportunity for equity in their home and hence a business investment. The problem in this case is not with a committee for repairs but with a busy husband who often does not have the time or know-how for the upkeep.

It is helpful if, at the time of moving in, the husband and wife make a list of all of the things that need to be done and place them in order of importance. Designate who is responsible—husband, wife, or outside help. It saves irritation if some dates for finishing each project can be agreed on. This gives checkpoints and a sense of accomplishment. Otherwise, it will be time to move on before you are moved in.

The main problem of decorating a minister's home becomes one of financing. One couple I know made a list of needs for furnishing their new home, and each time they received money for gifts or honorarium they immediately chose an item and went shopping to purchase it. Their home is beautifully furnished, and it was accomplished a little at a time.

Your home is what *you* make it.

Housekeeping is part of homemaking. "How can you stand to have your house ready for inspection at all times with people dropping in constantly?" the minister's wife is often asked. House inspectors are few. They are the types of persons who usually have a real need in their own lives. They are not in charge of your household, so receive them as any other guest. They might be simply looking for ideas. There should be no pressure on you for your house to have a non-lived-in look.

Give yourself time to accomplish your housekeeping. Organization is the key to this. A manager sees to tasks according to their importance. What is most significant to you? If you have a program of cleaning, washing, folding, putting away, ironing, window washing, closet and drawer straightening, there will be some personal satisfaction each day as you accomplish what you decide is critical.

An unmade bed takes two to four minutes to make, depending on how fast you are in the mornings. About two hours will see you through the house once or twice a week with a vacuum cleaner. A room of windows can be washed in ten to twenty minutes — inside one day — outside another day. About two hours of scheduled work each day will keep a house in order, even with extra help from two- and three-year-olds. The problem is not too much work. It is schedule, method of work, and how essential it is to you. We see the need of organization in all other endeavors, but somehow do not seem to realize that housekeeper exhaustion comes from lack of management in the housekeeping project.

One of the big problems in housekeeping is interruptions. The *telephone answering service* label is aided by a pad and pen by each phone. Write the message out. Do not get involved beyond the taking of the message unless you have the time. Some Christians look at the telephone as God's assignment for the day instead of a vehicle for rapid communication. Phone calls can be a temptation to lay aside your responsibilities and let your life drift into the pleasurable instead of the work assignment. Needs can usually be answered in a few minutes—then back to the housework.

There is also the interruption of drop-ins. In some cases they do not consider their work important, so they are ready for coffee and small talk before you have your breakfast dishes picked up, much less your kitchen cleaned.

This can be handled diplomatically by greeting her at the door with, "Come on in. We will have to rush this morning because I only have fifteen minutes for coffee." Do not try to explain yourself and all that you have to do. If she cannot accept the fact that you have other things to do, she will not be able to see that what you are planning to do is of much significance. Your neighbor is neither responsible for your day nor your supervisor.

This statement can be done in all kindness, with your remembering your time is your charge. A minister's wife can store up guilt and resentment at the same time when she feels she must let others do as they wish with her time. Other persons cannot waste your time unless you allow them to.

There are morning meetings that call for a rush to get off on time and leave many chores undone at home. You must return to them sooner or later. Plan ahead for those days. The career homemaker does.

There are those days that are broken into many small pieces by:

1. Children's staggered school times.

2. Small children at home—no naps—not time alone—messes to clean up.

3. Teaching children how to manage for themselves. There is always another lesson to be taught with small children.

4. Husband home for lunch.

5. Children home for lunch or on half-day sessions at school.

6. Errands or visits your husband has asked you to make.

The list is endless because there are always more things calling for attention than you may have time to do. This is why you must decide what is a good investment of time. Don't forget that you are the manager of your household. Others cannot and will not protect the use of your time. Since we are admonished to be good stewards of time, it behooves us to use it wisely and efficiently. Looking at each new day as God's personal gift will help you to value what you do with it.

Scheduling meals calls for a special system in a minister's home because of the quantity of appointments. A good part of the working day is involved in providing meals for the household. Have you considered how many skills are asked for in this area of responsibility?

The *planner*—What to have for breakfast, lunch, and dinner? Menu planning is one of the most difficult jobs but also one of the most rewarding. Planning ahead relieves the minister's wife of the nagging question, "What to have this meal?" A master list of what the family likes is an indispensable aid. It saves hours of staring into space and trying to remember what you had for dinner last Thursday evening. A big part of the direction is set when meals are planned, recipes are collected, and shopping lists are made.

The *shopper*—Shop for groceries with a well-planned list. Compose the list at the time of menu planning. This will save energy and money. If you guess at your grocery needs for a week, you will probably arrive home not knowing what to have for dinner. Or you may have failed to pick up something you needed.

When grocery shopping with small children, it helps to buy their treat either when you start or promise them when you have finished, depending on the time of day. Recently I observed a young mother and her small child at the checkout counter. The child had been given twenty-five cents. He had made his selections and checked out ahead of his mother and was waiting for her. She was teaching him how to shop; he was not just along for the ride but was participating.

It takes some financial expertise to provide well-balanced meals for a family today. Planning ahead saves dollars as well as time and tension.

The *cook*—With crock pots, microwave ovens, and automatic ovens, preparation is still necessary. It takes time to plan, serve, and clean up after a meal.

Many women do not like to cook—some because that is just not their thing, others because they have not learned how. If you fall in either of these categories, find someone who really enjoys cooking. Get better acquainted with her. She can teach you many interesting things and probably show you some shortcuts. Even if you don't seek outside assistance, decide now to begin to learn on your own. Experiment.

The trend of our day is *junk food*. Family members often eat at irregular intervals and odd hours. A wife needs to take the health of the family into consideration. Planning regularly balanced meals that provide the daily minimum requirements of nutrition for each member of your family will help accomplish this objective. We might even add the label nurse or doctor to your cooking skills and practice preventive medicine.

To a cook some of the world's most discouraging words are, "I don't like that" or "I don't want that tonight." My suggestion is that you serve your meals with a positive invitation to eat. "Come enjoy this good dinner of _____ that I have prepared for you." If no recognition or appreciation comes from the family, you have complimented yourself for the day, and you will have better digestion.

The *waitress*—Mealtime is a family time. It's one of the most important times of the day. Family meals should be close times, hopefully warm and friendly times. Jesus showed how he valued people as he went into their homes and shared the mealtime with them. The most important people in your life (the family) gather together at mealtime. Unfortunately, these occasions are becoming rare experiences in many homes. Families having meals together is deleted because of the outside pressures of urgency to get to other places and do other things.

The *maintenance supervisor or dishwasher*—falls under the category of housekeeper. Most of the time it is not the amount of time needed to do the task that bothers us, but that we must do it while other family members are relaxing. Part of the maintenance of the home is in the sharing of responsibilities. Attitudes can be cultivated very young when children are willing to help. If a mother cleans and straightens as she goes, there is little to be done. A mother and a father need to agree on who is responsible for a specific task and what training is needed. Sometimes it is easier and quicker to go ahead and do the task than to teach children. Being a part of the family means they have some tasks to carry out. A woman who keeps this part of her household running smoothly is very skilled and a good manager. It is the payscale that bothers her. We must be careful that we do not adopt the world's monetary standard to denote our worth as a homemaker.

The *efficiency engineer*—Time wisely and efficiently invested brings rich dividends. The home is a refuge for family relaxation. It's a haven to share our successes and failures, a place to love and be loved.

A manager of a smooth-running home will work the schedule for the good of all family members. Unrelated schedules are tearing the marriage and the family apart on a daily basis. A family cannot continually go in different directions and call the home more than a hotel. Management calls for time set aside where the needs of the marriage and family take precedence. There needs to be some time reserved for personal needs, your marriage relationship, and your children before the calendar is full of other requests. Otherwise you will be trying to build the most important relationships out of scraps of time.

The number 1 excuse I hear for not reserving family time is that families are never able to carry out their plans. Something unexpected always comes up at the last minute. There are not many actual interruptions of plans that are emergencies that cannot wait. Too often the problem is giving the family leftover time or a lack of planning. Appointments should be made and kept for marriage and family activities in the same way we make appointments with other people. If not, family members may feel ignored and build resentment toward God, the church, the home, and people in general.

Trying to schedule too many activities into a day causes a pressured and hurried atmosphere. Persons are more important than performance. We often give those around us the idea that God is only interested in what we accomplish and hardly interested in the person. Quite the opposite is true. We rush from one hurried project to another. We often give the impression we are performing our way to heaven. Relax. Obedience to God is fitting his plan into your lifestyle so that others see and desire what he has to offer.

The *hostess*—Occasionally I notice in a church bulletin that every activity is scheduled at the minister's home. It sounds almost like a clubhouse. Some people love to entertain. Others don't.

It is one thing to prepare the house for guests; it's another to always be responsible for all of the food and drink. Some congregations expect this. They can be tactfully educated to realize the cost and inconvenience. Some advanced planning such as, "The group can meet at my house if someone else will be in charge of the food" can solve a problem before it occurs. Sometimes I wonder who we expect to speak up for us and say what we are able to do and not to do. If we don't communicate our feelings, we can expect the unpleasant consequences that usually evolve into resentment.

If you have teenage children, it is quite natural for youth to congregate at your house. It is good for church youth groups to occasionally be invited to your home. They need to feel their importance to you by having the invitation to relate closely with you. The rare privilege that is afforded a minister and his wife of influencing youth by their genuine concern is irrefutable.

Your style of entertaining should be just that—your style. Be yourself. It makes the occasion more pleasant for you and for your guests. If your husband invites people in on the spur of the moment, consider this possibility in your weekly shopping activity. Have some instant foods on hand that can be prepared in a jiffy. Collect ideas for easily and quickly prepared foods. Put them on a card in your recipe box. Add new ones as you discover them. It is a secure, comfortable feeling to be prepared for such spontaneous times.

There are so many creative ideas for church families to have social activities in your home. In a sharing time at the annual retreat of ministers' wives in California, one of the women whose husband pastored a small church said she had a monthly birthday party in their home. It was a cake and punch affair for everyone who had a birthday that month. Persons observing recent birthdays brought their families. Another pastor and his wife enjoyed sponsoring a monthly dinner in the church fellowship hall in the form of a contributive dinner. A special cake was baked to fit the theme of the month for any with birthdays. Two different deacons and their wives served as host and hostess each month. These types of ideas can be socially stimulating.

In large churches there are many departmental activities that give special time for having groups together for fellowship. Such things as open house, teas, coffees, brunch, cook-outs, and picnics are some of the occasions that provide needed social togetherness. Remember to let your style of entertaining fit your personality and life-style.

Do not wait to have guests in your home until you have everything put together like Mrs. Elegant. The purpose of entertaining is to get better acquainted. It is an opportunity to share with each other. It is not a contest to see who can entertain in the grandest fashion. Because of various backgrounds, some find the task of entertaining guests in the home easy and relaxed. Most young wives will feel a bit of panic at first. A good rule is to keep it simple.

An older minister's wife, who has developed the fine art of receiving guests in a grand manner, shared her first experience of having another couple in for dinner. She fussed, worried, and worked for two days in preparation for the event. When the hour finally arrived, she accidentally let the turkey slide off of the platter onto the floor. The woman guest broke the tension by helping her recover the bird. The two women laughed and replaced the turkey on the platter. It was served as if nothing had happened.

Their secret formed a bond between them. They became the best of friends. That close association has continued through the years. The secret of these two women was finally revealed to help young ministers' wives. The older minister's wife reminded us, "Recover; regroup; nothing is as bad as it may seem. You will laugh about it later; why not now?"

The question of devoted friends for ministers and their wives is one that must be considered periodically. The need for social contact cannot be met in large groups of people. Everyone needs friends. Sometimes we use friends for the wrong purpose. Sometimes we're only seeking a person to unload on so we can feel better.

A friend is a person whom one knows well and is fond of, a supporter or sympathizer—one on the same side in a struggle.

We find an excellent example in the life of Jesus. He was available to the disciples; but Peter, James, and John sought a closer involvement with him than the others. He did not push them away but shared with them. In their closeness they were privileged to know him better. There are those in every congregation who will make opportunities to be closer to you. A friendship is formed and begins to grow. If nurtured the association develops into a mature, lasting relationship.

Problems can result many times from what is shared with friends. Intimate information should be kept confidential between a husband and a wife. A woman should not be talking with her best friend about things that should be discussed with her husband. Sometimes when a wife discusses a problem between her and her husband with a friend, she does not feel a need to talk about it with him. Marriages are not strengthened that way. Information about yourself is safe to share with a tried and true friend — who you are, what you feel, what you are working on, what your goals are, something you have learned. When we share intimate information about others, most of the time it comes close to *gossip*. It is usually flavored by how we saw it instead of how it really was.

We also burden friends with hurt feelings or anger that they can do nothing about when we talk about others. You may feel better temporarily, but she will feel worse. If you are actually seeking help on what you can do about ridding yourself from anger, that is different. She can help you to see yourself and may be able to offer a suggestion to help you. If you are looking for support for your point of view or to prove you are right, you will only be asking her to judge the other person guilty along with you. A listening friend can only be helpful to you when you are giving her accurate information about yourself.

When you wear the friend label, call for information about that person.

In conclusion, there are many more labels for the minister's wife that fit well under homemaker from dusting to laundry. She must cope with them. Remember, she has the option to arrange them according to her priorities. She can define them for herself.

Do not let yourself be forced into the mold of a previous pastor's wife. This potential problem is easiest handled not by negative resistance but by positive planning. In the beginning months of a new pastorate, there is time to establish yourself simply because you are a new person. Remember that you are you—that is great. What the new congregation needs is your freshness and originality.

There are many things that cannot be changed. It is easier but more costly just to be upset with what you cannot change than to take charge of yourself and work with those things that are changeable.

Boredom sets in when a wife ceases being responsible to change. A new hairstyle, new clothes, new reading material, or even new reading habits help to put variety in her life. She can choose different people to visit. She can dress up her meals. Try a different color of napkins on the table. There is only one reason for a person to be bored with her life: She doesn't want to do any changing. She wants *others* to do all the changing.

Working out the definition of homemaker takes effort and planning. A minister's wife can be comfortable with the label only to the extent that it fits her.

8
To Be or Not to Be

A professional is a person who does something with great skill or who is engaged in a specified occupation for pay or as a means of livelihood. The problem with this label worn by a minister's wife is not in the definition, but in the freedom to choose this label for herself. Many times she feels guilty pursuing her career. She does not feel free to see herself as she is and consider her own needs. The expectations of the congregation weigh heavily on her. In refusing to fit into a role mold, she may feel rebellious toward the congregation instead of responsible for her own choices.

Who is to decide if this identification is to be worn? Someone has said that there are three kinds of people: people-people, things-people, and idea-people. Our God-given abilities may be in many different directions. There are those of us who enjoy working with people. Others of us prefer furnishing the ideas. Still others excel in doing things. All are equally needed. None of us could accomplish much without the benefit of all three types of persons.

A lot of time and money has probably gone into the training of a person for a professional career. There is often a need for the minister's wife to use her knowledge and express herself in her particular field in order to help find fulfillment. We, as a group of minister's wives, must begin to give the privilege to each other to be ourselves. Even we are sometimes critical of each other when a minister's wife wants to go *her* own way. We feel she is not meeting her role expectations. Shouldn't that be left to husband and wife to decide?

One of the basic truths emphasized in the Bible is the need to love others as we love ourselves. Some ministers' wives need to give themselves the freedom to consider their own needs. A wife who fails to acknowledge where she is and tries to work from others' definitions of what her field of service is to be is in trouble with herself.

She will not have the freedom of service that comes from experiencing the abundant life. She will not be giving herself to others cheerfully but grudgingly. She must choose the amount and place to invest her time. Even if she enters professional circles, she will still be tagged a minister's wife and treated accordingly by most people.

A minister's wife in a large city who was an artist attended an advanced art class for over a year every week, established some friendships, and had a lot of pleasure in the exchange. One morning one of the ladies started talking about her husband and then asked my friend, "What does your husband do?" She answered, "He is a minister." There was a gasp, "A minister? I never dreamed you were a minister's wife!" From that point on there were comments to remind others that a minister's wife was present. If that kind of thing bugs you, there is really no way to get away from it. But it can be an advantage. My friend used it as an opportunity to share the Lord and his importance in her life. A career does have a way of putting a person on the cutting edge of witnessing at all times.

A married woman (wife) is not free to decide on a career alone. When she agreed to become a wife to her husband, she was saying that her life would be lived in relationship to his to accomplish marital unity.

There are many reasons for wanting to continue a career or to begin one. In order for agreement to come between a husband and wife, there is a need for input from both on an in-depth level. Complete honesty should be shared by both. A two-career marriage calls for role definitions being clarified, priorities determined, and an establishment of mutual goals.

There are several reasons for a minister's wife to pursue a career. Sometimes a woman does not feel good about herself or what she is accomplishing with her life. A new career label can provide her with a new area of identity that will help her feel better about herself. A career can help some women discover identity and meaning. However, a new label will not substitute for unfulfillment in her relationship with God, her husband, or her family. Some success in these basic relationships is primary for her to have a fulfilling life. A career does provide a new label, but it will not give meaning to her other labels. Being recognized for a job well done away from home does not automatically build a closeness with her husband and children. It must not be a substitute.

Is the need *money*? Inflation is jeopardizing family economy. Our standard of living has become more affluent even as a minister's family. It may be difficult to keep in step with the congregation and do what is expected on the salary received. There is an underlying need for extras for the family so that the children will not feel even more set apart from their peers.

Before a minister's wife gets a job and adds more stress to her life, a close look needs to be taken to see if the present income could be used more wisely. Will more money satisfy the lack or is the problem more than finances?

Before a wife begins an active career, there needs to be an accurate financial evaluation. One young minister and his wife found that they would actually be worse off financially after they added up all of the extra needs such as baby-sitting, clothes, transportation, meals out, and additional expenses related to her new job.

The question was asked me recently by a searching young couple, "Does being 'content in whatever circumstances I am' in in Philippians 4:11 mean giving up all of my ambitions?" These well-educated people were hurting financially. My response was, "Let's study and see what that passage says." We found that the Greek word for content (*autar´ kēs*) means self-sufficient, adequate, needing no assistance.

This passage of Scripture and other related passages give the picture of determining to use what you have to meet your own needs. Let's not forget that God is concerned with the needs of all of his children. The minister's wife is no exception. When the salary cannot be stretched to meet the needs, a full-time job outside the home may be the best option to see that provisions are adequate.

With some there is the need for a career *to get away from the position of minister's wife.* There are so many needless and useless demands made on her that the easiest answer is to remove herself so that she is not so readily available. The word no is one that seems wrong for her. She feels guilty if everyone is not happy with her performance. However, the person she is to seek to be pleasing to is God. This expression of following God comes as she works with her husband to be the best wife she can possibly be.

I hope the minister's wife never gets to the place that her directions from the Lord come only through what others want her to do. She must insist on retaining the option of saying no and give others the same privilege. This results in more joyful service on the part of everyone.

Statistics in the pastors' wives survey made by the Sunday School Board show that 44.8 percent of those minister's wives answering have a profession. Almost half of the women hold down two jobs— one in the home and one in the business world.

One of the greatest pressures is that of *trying to be two full-time persons* and sometimes three if she is a mother. There will of necessity need to be redefining of household responsibilities if the wife's health is to be protected and resentments avoided. If there are children in the home, they need to be included in the work plans so that they can participate as a part of the family. This is essential family planning and also a part of discipline. It helps children to feel that they belong, even though they may give static along the way.

If a wife fails to have the support of her husband and family in a career, she can easily fill up a cup of resentment from her anger that will take its toll on her attitude, joy, and energy. Two young children were discussing all the nice things their mother continues to do for them even though she is gone to work all day. The younger one stopped short, "She must have really been goofing off before." From a child's perspective, maybe—but a career woman is working two jobs because she feels it is her responsibility.

When a minister's family has financial needs, a part-time job that can be done on her own time may be the best approach. There are many small businesses operating out of the home that can bring in extra money. Be sure that the overall expense and profit is taken into consideration. You can end up making something like twenty-five cents an hour if you are not careful.

Whether the minister's wife chooses an extra job or business of just living on one salary, there needs to be a budget on which both partners work to make successful. With God's promises to provide, it can become a real challenging goal to live on what you receive. Children can be taught the value of money early in their lives, both how to earn and how to spend. There is an even greater lesson to be taught: what money will buy and what it will not buy.

Children can provide real pressure. Have a clear definition of what your responsibilities are to your children if you are going to seek a career. In other words, what is your definition of mother to each child where they are today in their development? When this is considered, a mother may see that she has a full-time career need of mothering at this time in her children's lives that she cannot hire others to do. When she deems it necessary to have a career outside the home, good care must be provided for the children. This helps relieve anxiety for their safety and resentment over the experiences she is missing.

Mother and Father need to be sure they have personal time with the children to assure the building of confidence, value, and love into their lives. Just being with children does not mean she is giving personal attention to them. A career need not prevent this personal attention. Some mothers who would not think of working outside the home do not give their children individual time. What you do in relation to your children takes planning and conscious effort.

The attitude of some church members can cause a minister's wife to feel added pressure. Occasionally a church member will expose prejudices of what a minister's wife ought to be when they say, "A minister's wife should not work. She needs to stay in her place." One minister's wife in this situation handled a comment like this with an invitation to that woman to have coffee with her. She questioned her further about what the place of the minister's wife was in her opinion. She helped the woman to see that her place was wife to her husband. It was helpful to both women and a matter of education.

Security can be another pressure to head into the work-a-day world. The lack of financial security in her husband's position causes some women to feel they must assume the role of providing for the household. Some women do this gladly and with the husband's approval and cooperation. They may be serving in a mission situation or working toward a better day. If the wife is trying to make up for the lack of the church providing an adequate income, there is a potential for resentment toward the church as a whole. Members who are responsible for the small salary may cause her anger. Many times she feels isolated from those who seem to her not to care for her family's welfare. To provide a livable income is the church's responsibility—not the wife's. This kind of a situation affects minister's children in a negative way the majority of the time. The wife and the children feel cheated. Many times a minister's self-esteem is under attack if he is made to feel he is not providing adequately for his family. This happens when a wife complains about the necessity of work because of the lack of income from the church. It also is done when members of the congregation complain about his wife not attending every meeting.

There is no need to labor under a false guilt because others feel a minister's wife should be doing something else. Lydia was able to contribute much to the furtherance of the gospel because of her wealth.

If a career is your choice, Martha Nelson has written a book *The Christian Woman in the Working World* that can be of help to you.

9
Right Perspective—Full View

Taking into consideration all the reflections behind all the labels of a minister's wife is packaged a very special person in a very special place. There is not another person who has a greater place to grow than the minister's wife. She is nestled in a group where the majority of the people genuinely care for her. She is sought out to counsel and to teach. She can be assured that her life counts as an influence.

I have spoken mainly to the difficult areas. There is little problem loving the lovable. It takes effort and choice to decide to work through complex areas.

A young friend of mine who has been doing an in-depth study of God's Word on rewards said to me, "After understanding how important everything we do is to God, I am glad I know his priorities. If I did not I would rush right past my husband and children and church and headlong into the world without stopping to know who I am."

If God is not the author of confusion, why is life so topsy-turvy much of the time? Order does not just happen. God has defined it, but we must personalize it and put it into practice. Just for starters, may I suggest the following order.

Most important relationship—God and I. Of all the labels there are to define, the most difficult one is *me.* This is at the top of the list in God's priorities. When he calls on me to relate to him on a one-to-one basis, I must of necessity identify myself. Identity comes by telling him who I am and who I am not. I call it prayer. It is also important for me to see my value to him.

If you want to bring about right action and thinking, it will have to come as you look at the investment God has made in you.

Think on things that are uplifting, and you will be exercising your faith. Praise will be the result. To discover more about self in a right

135

relation to the Lord, it is necessary to think about the things that are positive. One of the difficult times of my life was experienced when my late husband and I were told he had carcinoma of the colon and radical surgery had been performed. The Scripture that helped us gain our equilibrium was Philippians 4:8. We spent a day each listing all of the things we could on all eight positives listed in that verse. Positives are building blocks.

Do I have the freedom to be me? Yes, when God gives us freedom, we are free. The only one who can prevent identity is *you* if you refuse to recognize the material he has given you to work with or you try to live another's life. We must accept who we are before we know where to build from.

Second priority—two becoming one unit. When a husband and a wife are working on their marriage, the two of them present a stronger testimony. One of the greatest needs in the lives of many Christians today is to be able to see that a stable, growing marriage is possible.

There must be a pattern set for others to know that it is reasonable for two people to join together and be a working unit that satisfies the needs of both. A good working marriage provides a base for much greater and more effective service.

Do not try to assume responsibility for the marriage alone. Only be a wife. Define wife and share your definition with your husband for his input so that you can be more competent.

Third in line are children. Since children call for such a large block of time, it is important to live in a relaxed manner to keep from wearing yourself out physically and emotionally. The pediatrician gave one of my grandsons good advice when he was leaving the hospital at birth: "Be careful and don't wear your parents out because you don't get another set." Too bad he didn't understand. Children are a trust from God and are high on his priority list. Jesus said, "Let the children alone, and do not hinder them from coming to Me" (Matt. 19:14, NASB). They did not have physical needs like those Jesus had been healing that day, but he had time for them because they are important.

Defining the label "mother" and keeping it up to date could just be one of your most demanding tasks.

Another consideration should be the interest and care of the larger family (parents, sisters, brothers, etc.).

The church is a special relationship. If I would not be meddling too much, the unhappy minister's wife just might have her values out of sync with those God intends for her. I am not suggesting that she do less for God but that she harmonize her service with his Word. He is not the one who is pulling her apart.

What a privilege to be able to be a part of the body of believers and have a place of service.

Thank the Lord for those gifted persons who can make time to reach out to help a wider group of people. If you have special talent and time to train, this is an excellent place to invest some of yourself. The denomination needs to be considered a place of extended service as children become more self-sufficient.

My community—my opportunity to go into the world. The neighbors, schools, and community activities are areas where your testimony moves out into the lost world. Your relationship with God, husband, children, and church are noticeable here. There are many opportunities to help those who will never come to your church. Be real, and they will notice and desire to know your secret.

Several mornings when my husband and I prepared to go our separate ways for the day, he commented, "I am off to win the world—one at a time." As we are going, let's enlist others to help us. While we are busy we can train those around us; then *we* can win more *ones*.

Being overly concerned about how others see us hinders our availability to do simple everyday service because people *do* see us. Jesus wants people to see your good works and glorify your Father in heaven. The fact that others see something says God is working in your life in an effective way.

Think of God's structure as being as sound as a pyramid. The foundation is your involvement with God. This broad support furnishes room for a lifetime of growth. The marriage is built on that wide steady base. The children are placed in all that security. A stronger ability to make necessary provisions for the greater family is available. Rising on up, you add your care for other believers to the pinnacle of giving the message of God's love to those who are without

Christ. With this kind of arrangement we can stand with more confidence and assurance. God's love is established as it is exercised upward through the ranks from self to world.

Working under God's plan, I hope you will consider your many personal and ministry labels and carefully define them one by one to your own satisfaction. They will need review often to update them with the new material you discover about yourself.

To stand before a mirror and only look for areas that need to be corrected is disconcerting. Motivate yourself by seeing what you are doing right.

To build a productive life is similar to constructing a house. When you have decided what kind of a house you will erect, you then begin to gather the materials. Criticism of yourself is like buying your lumber for framing the house and cutting it into small pieces. Most of it would be wasted. What could be used would be weakened and much more expensive because each piece would have to be reinforced. Reflect on the things you see that you have going for you now. The house goes up quickly when you bring the building materials to the site and form them into your plans.

A brimming-over life is possible for each minister's wife as she sees the image of God in her mirror in her hall as she comes into and goes out of her home.

May God bless and keep you as you do an even greater *unique* service for him.